Lisa Carducci

AS GREAT AS THE WORLD

With illustrations by Lao Du

CHINA
INTERCONTINENTAL
PRESS

About the Author

Lisa Carducci, born in Canada, earned a M.A. in Linguistics and completed the Ph.D. programme from the University of Montreal. After a career in teaching, in Canada and China, she worked for the Overseas (French) Programmes of CCTV, and is now working for *Beijing Review*.

She has written more than 30 books in four languages, and almost 2,000 articles on a variety of topics, published in several countries.

In 2001, she was granted the Friendship Award of the People's Republic of China.

↑ Old lane at first sight.

↑ The merciless character "*chai*" (Beijing, Xidan).

↓ Discovering life in a Beijing *siheyuan*.   ↓ Learning from Ronald.

→ Door Guardians and couplets to welcome the year of the Horse 2002.

← Tibetan children reading the *Beijing Children's Weekly*.

↑ Horse Race festival in Anduo, North Tibet

→ Planting trees with a group of volunteers.

← Contemplating contentment (Xiahe, Gansu).

↓ Birds on an outing to the park.

↑ Monks don't just pray.

↑ Enjoying a local speciality in Mizhi (Shaanbei).

The author and her husband Du Jinsu at Zhenbei Tai (Shaanxi).

(Photos by Du Jinsu, Olga Cassetta, Lisa Carducci and Xie Feng)

As Great as the World

Contents

Introduction

Three reasons led me to China: curiosity, writing, and teaching. The first time was in 1985. My study in linguistics placed me on the path to the Arabic and Chinese languages. Which of these two would I learn? I was hesitant. If I was interested in Arabic poetry, I had never, on the contrary, approached Chinese culture. Before deciding, I thought I would see for myself – in the country itself – what did these people look like?

So I went to China... and fell in love with the land at first sight. A "coup dc foudre"! It seemed incomprehensible to spend only one month in this country – in this world, I should say – where there was so much to discover. I wanted to live here for at least one year. Back in Montreal, I offered my skills to the World University Services of Canada, which then would have found me a teaching position, but this escaped me at the last moment. Probably, the time was not yet right.

In 1989, I was on my sabbatical and dedicated that time to painting and writing *Stagioni d'amore* (Seasons of Love), a novel about reincarnation. One of the four lives I describe is set in China. Just as I had been to the other countries in the book – Italy, France, and Canada – I wanted to do the same for the Chinese section, and I landed here on February 14, Valentine's Day. I went back on May 31.

In October 1990, I applied for a position in Poland, and was immediately accepted. Meanwhile, I asked myself, "Why Poland, since I've always wanted to go to China?" I advised the Polish organisation that I would sign a contract at the last minute and only if I didn't receive an invitation from China, as China was my first choice. Things were clear. The deadline was June 3. Well, on June 3, at 10:00, the postman brought a registered letter: the invitation from a foreign language university in Beijing.

Didn't Einstein say – rightly so – that events wait for us? This is what some call chance, luck, or destiny.

And here I am in Beijing. I immediately felt at home. Moreover, I am Italian on my father's side, and was born in Canada; I had till then spent my life divided between two worlds – my body in Canada and my spirit in Italy. I don't know how the miracle happened, but once in China, I felt, for the first time in my life, repatriated. My soul and body were in the same place. This feeling was so satisfying that I wanted to prolong it, until my roots had deepened in the soil of the Middle Kingdom.

Of the 30 books I've written so far, two-thirds were published after I arrived in China and half concern China or are inspired by her. Poetry, novels, short stories, essays – I wrote first in French or Italian, but my recent works are in Chinese or in English. I also have written almost 2,000 articles in newspapers and magazines of a dozen countries. At every opportunity, I speak of "my" China. Just as a couple's love depends on respect, I believe that wars result from a lack of respect between nations, and such lack originates from ignorance. China has given me so much that I cannot remain silent. I will then share with you, Readers, my humble experience. It will remind you of memories, make you smile, surprise or even shock you ... perhaps. I don't pretend to bear the truth, since truth belongs to each person as he or she perceives it. What I wish to do is to invite you to reflect, in order to have a better understanding of China, this exciting China, an extraordinary land.

The Daily Life of a Foreign Expert

Housing

Let's go back to 1991. At the Foreign Language Institute No. 2, as it was then called, I had a furnished apartment in the foreign professors' building on campus. I especially appreciated the large front and back balconies that allowed me to grow tomatoes, basil, garlic, and even green beans in pots. I was fond of my apartment, which was very comfortable during summer, but winter seemed so long, because we had heat from 6:00 to 8:00 a.m., since we were supposed to be in class then, and in the evening, until 10:00, when it was time to go to bed. In the afternoon, if we stayed home to prepare lessons or mark the students' work, we had to tolerate the biting cold that found its way through our woollens, scarves, and gloves (even inside, yes!), because there was no other way to heat the place. It was the same for hot water: two hours in the morning and three hours at night. The classrooms were not heated, either. We had to keep our coats, boots, and gloves on while teaching. It was still tolerable for the teachers, who could stand and move around, but the students, who were seated and immobile, would freeze on the spot.

A new building was constructed and I spent my second teaching year there. It was modern, well-lit and... overheated. Windows – had architects forgotten about us humans? – were sealed shut and students would fall asleep during class probably because of the lack of oxygen and fresh air.

Also, when in 1993, I moved to the Friendship Hotel following a change of work, I could not rid myself of a reflex: associating the faucet to the clock. I programmed any activity that required water, such as showering or washing my hair or clothes to the clock. How good it was to enjoy hot water 24 hours a day again, just as I had before coming to China!

The Friendship Hotel is a State establishment, where foreigners enjoy comfort and protection. It was for our protection from intruders that the Chinese were not allowed to enter without a clear invitation. When a friend visited, we had to go to the main entrance and confirm that person's arrival. At the entrance of each apartment building, the visitor, accompanied by his or her host, had to sign and leave an ID card. At 22:30, all visitors had to be out or a call from our "caretakers" would remind us – and sometimes not too delicately.

The *Yayuan*'s (Garden of Elegance) "red gate" is, for me, a symbol of the reform and opening-up policy so often mentioned since 1980. I had the chance to experience the most dynamic phase of it, the last decade of the 20th century. In 1993, the gate I had to pass to enter my living compound was closed and locked at 23:00. If a resident returned late, he or she would humbly ask the night staff to open the red gate. One day, the door was closed at 23:00, but not locked. A year or two later, it was only half-closed, then, not at all, and finally, in 1999, it was left open. For the old residents, this "space" remains the "red gate." Sometimes, we designate an appointment to a newcomer at the "red gate"; he or she seeks it but will never understand.

Transportation

During my first trip in China, one of the images that most impressed me is the number of **bicycles**. In 1997, I went to Amsterdam. A friend took me to a bridge, stopped, and waited for my reaction. "What am I supposed to say, or see?" I asked. He pointed to the bicycles. "Oh! You forgot that I live in China. This is nothing new to me."

What impressed me most about the Chinese bicycles is that they were all uniformly black, of the same size, and the same model. At that time, people didn't steal bicycles, so there was no need to lock them up.

Before coming to Beijing I had never ridden a bike, except for a few disastrous attempts that had left bruises as large and dark as big eggplants on my body. But, once here, to do as everyone else, I tried to learn. I rode only on campus grounds, from one building to another. Only once did I dare to pass the gate and ride on the street toward the post office. I didn't pay attention to the distance, which was covered in a few minutes, and even passed the post office to continue for 3 or 4 kilometres before making a U-turn. But, one thing I realised is that I was a public danger on my "vehicle" and that I had better give it up.

At those times, bicycles were used to transport the whole family: father on the saddle, mother on the back, with the baby in her arms or in the bamboo seat in front of the handle bars.

There were as many bicycles as citizens in the city but this has changed. Cars have begun to wander into the bicycle paths, polluting them, and drivers use their horns at the cyclists to let them pass. Little by little, under the policemen's eyes, the situation has returned to normal.

In Shanghai, bicycles are considered a public nuisance, and the municipality tries all means to get rid of them. The bicycles don't cause pollution or noise, they occupy little space, and they contribute to a person's health. Should we see such a favourable species unjustly condemned to extinction?

I had left Beijing in 1989, and when I returned two years later, my initial surprise was in seeing how the number of **cars** had multiplied, surpassing mules and luxury tourist buses. I thought it would be catastrophic if the Chinese people, in this city of 10-12 million, ever bought private cars. Well, this disaster is being realized. Between 1995 and 1999, serious parking problems arose; cars invaded the sidewalks of the largest streets and the *hutong* (lanes), and the pedestrians no longer had the right of way. Meanwhile, corrective measures have been adopted, parking lots have been built, and order has been restored. But, with so many cars, the city now resembles a North American metropolis.

While I personally thought the State should ban the rising number of cars, it did the contrary. According to the national development plan, the automobile is considered to be an economic pillar, which is understandable, considering how many people it feeds, directly and indirectly. Work units are encouraged to provide cars for their employees, and individuals are encouraged to buy private cars, which the Chinese call the "family car," distinct from a "work unit car."

Following China's WTO entry (which made car prices drop), the Northwest Information News survey on 22,800 consumers in 57 Chinese cities shows that 12% of the participants in the survey plan to buy a car, and 29% of these potential buyers will do it with a bank loan.

It's tolerable, as long as the traffic flow can be improved; the number of buses and bus lines has increased dramatically. A city staff member said that the bus route map in Beijing needed to be adjusted every 20 days on average in 2000 to accommodate the frequent changes.

Moreover, a lane is now reserved for buses in the main streets. Many other measures may be borrowed from large, modern cities in the world. For instance, private cars and taxis could be fined if they carry just one passenger; access to downtown could be restricted; parking lots could be reduced or their prices raised; priority could be given to bicycles and buses in cities; and a heavy fine should be given to those driving in bicycle lanes. Some of these measures are being examined or already have been implemented, but at this moment the patient runs faster than the doctor.

The construction of the Fourth Ring Road has been completed. Some of the Third Ring Road's entrances and exits have been rebuilt for more efficiency, and the Fifth Ring Road is already under construction.

Due to the number of cars (and inexperienced drivers), traffic accidents increased significantly, I think, between 1996 and 1999; after, strict policies were adopted. Aimed at protecting the citizens' lives, the tall, sturdy medians prevent people from crossing the streets except at the crosswalk or bridges and underground passages; traffic lights have been installed, and traffic agents (although insufficient in number) make hurried pedestrians and drivers wait for their turn to cross.

Nevertheless, the average Chinese driver is in my eyes, at a very low level. In China, everything may oceur on the roads, as long as no policeman is visible. For example, a person can be seen departing suddenly from a private driveway and then cutting into regular traffic to melt into the main stream. Drivers who make turns never give priority to pedestrians who cross the street correctly. Some drivers pass cars on the right, and so on. Also, when a licence is granted, a new driver often has not yet practised in the streets, but only on the driving-school grounds.

The number of **taxis** shot up during the decade following my arrival in China. They numbered 16,000 in Beijing in 1991, then 57,400 two years later, and 90,000 in 1997. At the end of

1998, there were 1,000 taxi companies in the capital. Since the cost remains relatively low, taxis are accessible to almost everyone.

Even though acts such as refusing to drive a passenger and cheating on the price are less evident today, some taxi drivers still won't use the meter on routes where they will not find passengers on the return, such as the downtown-to-airport route. They prefer to impose a surcharge, especially to the foreign customers who shut their eyes to the language, rules, distances, itineraries, and cost.

First, for the sake of maintaining order, at the Beijing West Railway Station (*Xikezhan*) and at the old Beijing Station, only the 1.6 yuan* taxis are authorized to queue for customers. Their drivers must pay 1 yuan to the person who allows them to take passengers. A real little mafia! If the customer wants the meter to be used, the cost is always higher than for the same distance in the reverse direction. The meter is circumvented.

The customer who asks for a receipt can report the facts to the taxi company. Complaints are always well-received, and the guilty party will soon offer an excuse and refund the cheated client. Very few foreigners use this form of consumer protection, because they don't speak Chinese or because, being tourists, they ignore the existence of this right, but mostly because they think that, even with an increase, the cost is still lower than the one they would pay in their own countries. What about the Chinese then? "They are too indifferent," said a taxi company owner.

Second, when leaving the railway station from the north exit, taxis can only go east. At the central station, the first two kilometres just brings one back to the south of the station by a long detour if one wishes to go west, north, or south.

Finally, if the customer wants to take a 1.2 yuan taxi, he or she has to walk a long distance, carrying the luggage, because these cheap taxis are not allowed to pick up clients at the station or close to it.

---

* 1 yuan = 0.12 USD or 0.14 EUR.

But not all taxi drivers are dishonest. On the contrary! Some bring back, without charge, items left by their customers in their cars: wallets, cellular telephones, portable computers, and briefcases.

Since the beginning of 2002, some taxis in Beijing are crowned with a red star light, a reward for humanitarian behaviour or even heroic act, given to a few elite drivers.

Especially since Beijing has won the right to organise the 2008 Olympic Games, more and more drivers (and other public workers) are trying to learn English and attend evening classes or talk with their foreign customers.

Environmental protection policies have multiplied quickly in recent years, especially before and after Beijing bid's for the Olympics, one result being that the use of the vehicles known as *miandi* (breadloaf-shaped) was discontinued in 1998, because their design could not accommodate unleaded gasoline.

The safety belt became compulsory in 1993. It's not surprising to see drivers and passengers to avoid buckling up; nevertheless, they are fined. All the countries that imposed it before went through a similar phase of resistance, which seems to be a normal human reaction.

City transportation was so arduous a decade ago; **buses** were always overloaded, like furnaces in summer and freezers in winter. The window panes were often broken or missing. The vehicle seemed like a huge clanking mass of noise, and one wondered if the bus would arrive at the terminal in one piece. Without exaggeration, the people lining up to get on the bus mostly seemed like a disordered crowd – as usual in China – of a hundred or more exasperated passengers. To get on an already crowded bus, one had no other way than to push, in order to help those in front to climb on board, and to be pushed, in order to let the door close. The less nimble and/or audacious had to wait for the next bus, and often let many others pass through.

The most onerous means of transportation and maybe the most squalid, the public bus remains my favourite because I consider it absolutely essential for discovering the Chinese urban life. Taking a bus in Beijing is an event, an experience beyond comparison! Even though in certain places there are marked designations to keep people in line or even though persons with red flags force people to keep order, when the passengers see the vehicle's silhouette in the distance, they will throw themselves into the street and start to push. Those near the front also push to ensure that they will get a seat.

Service has become increasingly faster in recent years with more buses, and no more than 4-5 minutes waiting time. Considering that there are 7-8 million daily users, one can say that the population is well-served. Taking a bus means learning to fight, to make one's way among the passengers to buy a ticket as well as to get off without being pushed inside by the crowd trying to get on. On the one hand, to push; on the other hand, to accept... as one has just done to the others, in order to get on the bus and because it's the only way to get on during the rush hours. Nevertheless, one might say that the morning rush hour extends to 10:00 and the noon rush hour starts at about 11:00 and lasts till 13:30, while the end of workday rush hour starts around 15:00.

Throughout the years, new buses have emerged and the old ones have disappeared. The bus lines that are used the most are double deckers and cost a little more to ride but people always get a comfortable seat.

In July 1997, air-conditioned vehicles were put into service in the summer, with heat in the winter.

The public transit system loses money. The State injects billions of yuan every year. Despite a rise of 250%, as in 1996, the price of tickets is still much lower than the actual cost.

The Beijing **subway** opened in 1970 and works reasonably, and the lines are extending continuously. In 2010, the network will be completed with its 15 lines, and what presently covers 43 km will cover 408. In the capital city, the subway transports 1.5 million users daily. At rush hour (18:00 to 18:30), a train passes every 30-60 seconds.

Important improvements are needed to upgrade the Beijing subway to the level of an international subway. For instance, the ticket selling system, of selling each ticket individually, and the human checking are very obsolete. It's impossible to buy a ticket book in advance. There are no vending machines, either, and no magnetic cards, as in Shanghai. Signs at the different exits, designating the main areas and spots that can be found outside, such as a museum, park, large store, university, bus lines, and so on, are also absent. When they do appear, they are incomplete, or far from the actual exit (often, one has to backtrack and face the crowd to go back in the opposite direction), or are only in Chinese.* A benefit in the Beijing subway is the washrooms at each station and since March 1, 2002, the fee to use them has been waived.

Along with the public transit system in many cities are the **minibus** services that follow the same route. Each car sits 20 people. A few years ago, the ticket was 10 to 20 times more than the bus ticket, but then bus price rose while the minibus price remained the same. In 1996, smokers lost their

* Remarkable improvements concerning signs at the exits have taken place in August 2002. But the cardinal directions are no more indicated, the exits being identified only by A, B, C, D.

privilege on a minibus, except when the operators themselves smoked. The quality and cleanliness have improved. Each vehicle is now identified by a luminous sign on top, and, since 1997, signs there are to indicate where they can stop to avoid the confusion they used to cause in the traffic. But, at the beginning of this century, since many transport companies have appeared in Beijing, these minibuses serve only the outskirts or have become shuttles between downtown and the new housing complexes far away.

The **train** has always been the most important means of transportation for long distances for the Chinese people, but the railways and the trains themselves are not enough for the millions of passengers who travel in this immense country, and some provinces such as Guizhou or the Xinjiang Uygur Autonomous Region are not covered by the train or their railways are insufficient due to extremely difficult geographic conditions. However, Tibet will be linked to Qinghai by the

Golmud-Lhasa line. Construction began in late June 2001, proof of extraordinary intellect, creativity, and willpower.

Each year, the train quality improves visibly, and the speed, obviously. The Beijing-Urumqi time decreased twice recently, from 72 hours to 60, and then to 48. Beijing-Shanghai can be covered in 12 hours instead of the previous 21, which was not long ago.

About ticket reservations: before, one had to spend hours at the station to hear when his or her turn would come, or that there were no seats available. Today, points of purchase are distributed all around the city. A ticket can be bought 2-3 days in advance, depending on the time of year and destination. It's also possible to buy through the Internet, with a little patience. The most important of the above is that the points of purchase now are linked by computer, which may seem common in a developed country, but it's still new in China. This means that, if the West Station says there are no more tickets, it's fruitless to run to the Central Station to see if there are any left. The most serious problem is still not being able to buy a return ticket, except on some special itineraries, which are being tested presently. So, when one travels, especially during festivals or holidays, he or she knows the departure time but not the time of return.

Airplanes were once a prerogative of the foreigners because of their high price. Since taking a plane is often the only way to go back on time when the trains are overcrowded, and since the earnings of the Chinese people have increased, there is no longer any difference between the Chinese and foreigners. Anyway, planes can be sold out of seats, just as well as the trains.

One should note that foreign experts paid by China had a white (privilege) card before (then yellow, and later orange), when the admission in museums, parks, monuments, the train and plane tickets, and hotel rooms differed between the local population and the tourists. Our foreign expert card allowed us foreigners to pay less than a tourist but still more than a Chinese citizen. The same card also allowed us to pay in *renminbi* or local money (yuan) some services that visitors or foreigners working for embassies or foreign enterprises were obliged to pay in FEC (Foreign Exchange Certificate), before the reform in 1994.

Privileges

Even though foreign experts have been losing, year after year, many privileges once included in their contracts, they still enjoy free housing, a non-negligible right, considering the price of apartments – rented or purchased.

Before, foreign experts had special transportation to the downtown area two or three times a week, but this service was discontinued. Actually, it is no longer necessary; since public transportation has improved and salaries have increased, foreign experts now prefer to go out on their own and at their convenience.

Besides, the reform of enterprises requires each work unit to reduce expenses if it can't earn more. It's therefore normal that foreign experts take a part in this process. When all was free before, they now pay for gas (a tank was 16 yuan a decade ago and 47 today), and telephone expenses; medical fees are no longer completely covered; the holiday allowance is no longer given out if the foreign expert returns to the home country during this period, etc. Most important is that the Chinese government units are increasingly reluctant to hire persons who come to China with their spouses and children.

When this is the case, dependants are not covered by the employer under many circumstances. Chinese units prefer to hire single people and to choose them among the foreigners who are already in Chinese territory, sometimes sacrificing quality at the cost of a plane ticket.

For the Chinese media or education fields, hiring a foreign expert is not easy. Even if a copy of the diploma, recommendation letters, and a test are scrutinized, it's still difficult to know if the candidate is serious and truly competent. Moreover, nothing is known about his or her personality. Why does this person want to come to China? How does he or she work? Does this person get along well with colleagues? Does he or she have a cooperative spirit? In teaching fields, especially, too many so-called professors have been hired, just because they could speak this or that language, thinking that they could teach it. Some were much too young and only thought of having fun, going out every night, returning after the gates were closed, and jumping over them, laughing. Others were unemployed in their country, so why not try China? Others – unfortunately, more than one dares to imagine – had just gone through a love affair that they wanted to forget "at the end of the world," often at the expense of naive young Chinese girls, who believed these gentlemen who promised to marry them, take them to their dream countries, and shower them with worldly goods.

On the other hand, if the privileges continue to shrink, the foreign experts' situation in China will continue to be less interesting, and if their salaries, even with occasional raises, don't increase as quickly as the Chinese population's (they are inferior to many Chinese people's revenue presently), China will risk having a contingent of unqualified persons, without experience; people who, for personal reasons or national reasons in their own countries, have not found jobs.

Let's talk about the remaining privileges. Previously, performance tickets cost 8 or 10 yuan; today, they're at least 200 or 300 yuan and are offered three or four times a year, for a ballet, concert, variety show, or for special occasions such as National Day, and they are given to us foreign experts by our work units. Even for Christmas, which is not a Chinese holiday, we foreign experts are invited to a banquet where even the most critical person can't find fault. It's touching to see how much the Chinese people worry about us when Christmas is arriving; as we are far from our family; they compensate with gifts, cards, and generous heartfelt gestures. They show their friendship and gratitude.

Some details may seem insignificant, but they show the kindness of the Chinese people toward their "precious guests." For example, only when someone brought it to my attention did I realise that, at the Friendship Hotel, there is no apartment 13, 113, 213 in the buildings where the foreigners live, since the number 13 is considered to be bad luck. Chinese persons, instead, avoid the number 14, which is pronounced "*yao si*" (one, four), a homophone of "to die soon."

Also, the foreign experts' apartments are heated two or four weeks (according to the years) before the official date of November 15 and beyond March 15, dates imposed by the municipality of Beijing and appropriate according to the local climate.

Finally, since 1991, National Day is the time that the State bestows 40 foreign experts with the Friendship Award for their outstanding contribution in the development of China or the friendship between China and other countries. This is the highest decoration that the State may give a foreigner and, in 2001, I had this honour.

Festivities

When I was a schoolgirl in a Catholic school, I had to memorise the dates of the 45 most important days of the religious calendar: Saint Joseph, patron of the craftsmen; Saint Anna, protector of the pregnant women; Saint Cecile, patronne of the musicians, etc. But these were not celebrated. No holiday, no special dishes, no unique ceremonies. In China, I was surprised at first by the celebratory spirit of the Chinese people and by the number of their festivities: national, ethnic, religious, agricultural, folkloric.

Chinese people first offered **Christmas** to the foreign experts hired by China and who were living far from their own countries and families. They did so as a kindness, imagining what it would have been like for them to spend Spring Festival alone, for example, far from their loved ones.

When I taught, I was allowed to take time off, but my students had to go to the classroom and work, "unless your foreign teacher allows you to celebrate the occasion," the dean told them. Students themselves were not allowed to organise a Christmas party, but their participation in foreigners' celebrations was tolerated, because they were seen – rightly so – as a means to deepen the knowledge of Western culture. It was my pleasure, then, to have them at my place, where we cooked together and sang in French Christmas carols that they knew better than I; we exchanged gifts and played group games.

Also, even when expressed awkwardly, the gestures and behaviour of the Chinese people are very touching, but even more than the Chinese friends and colleagues, the work units pay great attention to Christmas for their foreign experts, and, each year, between Christmas and New Year's Eve, they organise a banquet. Nevertheless, in the Chinese minds, there is Spring Festival for them and Christmas for everyone else. A Canadian who teaches in Nanjing told me that, with the greatest goodwill in the world, his university had set great festivities for the non-Chinese teachers and students, 95% of whom were Korean and Japanese, who had never celebrated Christmas before.

Often, over the years, in order to have free time on December 25, I've worked late on Christmas Eve. I was always amazed to see my Chinese colleagues leave the office early on the 24th, wishing me a joyous "Merry Christmas!" passing in front of my door as they rushed to meet their friends for a Christmas party. But, I repeat, Christmas is not a Chinese festive day.

Foreigners also have the opportunity to celebrate Chinese festivities, of which **Spring Festival** is the most important. In the north of the country, people prepare *jiaozi*, a thin dough crescent that they place in one hand and fill with eggs, tofu, meat, cabbage, shrimp, *jiu cai* (chives), and then finish off in different shapes, according to their creativity and "talent." *Jiaozi* made by foreigners are easy to distinguish among those made by experienced Chinese people! It's customary to eat *jiaozi* during the first 15 days of the new year. As all kinds of *jiaozi* are now available frozen in supermarkets, will the young generation keep the home-made *jiaozi* tradition? Many Chinese people in their 20s admit to never having made any. Moreover, old traditional dishes prepared especially for each occasion are now available all year long, and the festivities' charm is fading away.

Traditions related to Spring Festival vary from north to south and from city to countryside. In large cities, people can take part in several recreational activities or see performances in public parks. In Beijing, for instance, there is an annual "temple fair," a popular cultural event that is organised around five major temples.

The new year celebrations last till the 15th day of the Lunar Year. In the countryside, each single day is assigned a special activity. For example, the first day, people stay at home. The second day, they visit the elderly; the next, they visit former teachers, etc. I spent the last *Chunjie* (Spring Festival) in the north of Shaanxi Province. There, traditions are still truly alive. As it's not a tourist place, all the stores, hotels and even restaurants were closed for 15 days. People just enjoyed themselves, watching street performers, such as the *yangge* group dancers or *yaogu* (belt drum) players.

The festive period ends with the **Lantern Festival**. On that day, *yuan xiao* (glutinous rice balls stuffed with fruit paste and other tasty things) are enjoyed. Lanterns are placed everywhere, usually made of paper or silk. The ones the children make at school are of Sprite and Coca-Cola plastic bottles. Red paper banners are stuck on each side of the doors. On these the grandfather or the family poet has carefully written in black or gold ink what are called couplets. These words or sentences are a *leitmotiv* for the family, and the red paper will remain until the sunshine bleaches them, the rain soaks them, and the wind tears them off.

The **Mid-Autumn Moon Festival**, in September, is the first festivity I experienced in China. It is a family reunion first of all; from every part of the country, people go to their hometowns to celebrate. It's said that the mid-autumn moon is the brightest of the year, and some also say "the roundest." The round shape of the moon and the round shape of the fruits and of the *yue bing* (moon cakes) that over time have become square for practical reasons (even square watermelons are produced for easier transportation) symbolise the family circle.

Yue bing vary from region to region. Generally round and about 8 cm in diameter, they are baked in reverse in a mould that prints decorative patterns and wishes on top, or describes

their filling. In Beijing, they are stuffed with red bean paste or dried fruit. In other places, they may contain pork or chicken, sugar, coconut, laurel flowers, honey, egg yolk (even two of them), lotus seeds, chestnut paste, peanuts or walnuts, etc. Personally, I like them more and more each year, but I realise that most of the foreigners don't appreciate them at first. "It's... special...," they say. The taste may seem odd when one is not used to it, but if one persists, he or she may become addicted to them.

On October 1, **National Day**, which underlines the anniversary of the founding of the People's Republic of China, in 1949, and May 1st, or Labour Day, are celebrated with exquisite performances in theatres; others, on television, and, in addition are a variety of activities, excursions, reward ceremonies, parades, fireworks, and banquets. No one would think of staying at home and resting in bed on such a day.

Several days before National Day and Labourers Day, hundreds of thousands of potted flowers come out from all greenhouses (each work unit has one, generally), and are installed, in just a few hours, along the streets, in the State building staircases, in front of universities and enterprises. The decoration may be completed with a fountain. Wishes are written along with the flowers. Tian'anmen Square is absolutely grandiose on these occasions, with a different thematic decoration every year. Therefore, many couples take advantage of these two holidays, weather permitting, to celebrate their weddings, and take photos in a wonderful setting.

The *Qingming* or Pure Brightness Festival is a day to commemorate the dead. As almost everywhere in the world, Chinese people, especially in large cities, don't mourn their dead in black or white clothes anymore, but in the countryside the tradition of a funeral procession and of hired weeping mourners (women paid to cry at the funeral) are still alive, and one can see whole families wearing white clothes, with a hemp rope as a belt and a large white band on their foreheads.

The *Qingming* is also designated as the cold meal day for the legend that surrounds its origin 2,000 years ago. That day, families visit their beloved ones' tombs and clean them. Then they burn symbolic money, and paper cars and houses, as well as all the things that the dead might need in the other world. Finally, before leaving, they leave food.

Han people, the largest ethnic group in the country (91. 59% of the Chinese population) also celebrate the *Chong Yang*, or Double-Nine because of its date, the 9th day of the 9th month. This 2,000-year-old festivity is based on an interesting legend. A Taoist master had predicted to Huang Jing that bad luck would strike his family on the 9th day of the 9th month, unless each member of his family climbed the mountain and drank chrysanthemum wine, carrying with them a little bag full of chrysanthemums. So Huang Jing did this with his family. But when they returned home, they found their dog, their chicken, and pigs all dead.

Medicinal virtues are attributed to the chrysanthemum. Soaked in yellow wine, this flower may sharpen one's vision, cure dizziness, and ease arterial tension. A sudatory, it warms the digestive system and balances one's energy. Its leaves can heal cholera, and its roots keep the mosquitoes away.

The chrysanthemum, appreciated for its 200 varieties (of which 180 exist in Beijing), includes ox-eye daisy, blue chrysanthemum, little daisy, and sweet-william. It has been recognized for 3,000 years in China and lauded in songs by poets and artists for centuries for its delicate hues: purple, orange, yellow, white, and its lacy configurations.

Another local festival, based on a flower, is the **Luoyang Peony Festival** in Henan Province, during the second half of April. According to the legend, the Tang empress Wu Zetian had two lovers. One day, all three of them took a walk in the garden, but it was winter. Therefore, the Spring goddess was summoned to make the flowers blossom during the night.

The flowers didn't dare disobey the empress. The next morning, Wu Zetian found 100 blooming flowers in the garden, except a peony that had defied the empress's will. To punish the flower, Wu Zetian ordered that all the peonies be transplanted to Luoyang. From that day, Luoyang has been their home, and the peonies have never failed to honour their realm.

Among the ethnic festivals, the **Water Splashing Festival** is certainly the most well-known. It marks the New Year of the Dai, an ethnic group in Yunnan. According to the legend, a ferocious demon who was hated by his seven wives was killed by the seventh to whom he had revealed his weakness: "The one who picks a hair from my head and places it around my neck will kill me." The woman didn't need him to repeat it. During the night, she cut off his head with one strand, but the head, upon hitting the ground, was set on fire; then, after rolling into the river and making the water boil, all the fishes died. She tried to bury it, but the smell was so nauseating that she, somehow unable to get rid of her husband's head, had to hold it in her arms. When she grew too tired, she was relieved by the other wives in turn.

The women used this time of rest to thoroughly wash and cleanse the blood from their hands and clothes. Now, people remember the seven heroines by splashing water on themselves. The first day of the festival is dedicated to dragon-boat races; the next day, to the water ritual, and the evening, to artistic performances.

The elderly are splashed with moderation, with olive tree branches bathed in water or by pouring a few drops of water from a spoon on their heads, which indicate wishes for good health. But young people empty buckets of water on each other until they are completely soaked. The wetter one becomes, the happier he or she will be through the year.

As an example of a festival that strayed from its ethnic origins, let's talk of the 5th of the 5th lunar month, or *Duanwu jie,* on which the Chinese prepare *zongzi* (pyramid-shaped rice cakes wrapped in reed leaves), and attend the dragon-boat races.

In Jingzhou, Hubei Province, the ancient capital of the Chu Kingdom, the international dragon-boat races takes place annually. The largest dragon boat in the world is 69 m long by 2.38 m wide and 70 cm deep. It weighs 23 tons and can accommodate 178 persons.

Seven thousand years ago, men dug out tree trunks and slid them onto the water and navigated with two wooden oars. Men then considered the dragon as their protector and carved its image on everyday objects, as well as on their boats. Little by little, dragon-boat races were organised as a way to please the dragon and obtain its benediction. Finally, the whole boat was transformed into a dragon.

The origin of these races can be found in the Chu Kingdom history: "Seeing Qu Yuan, great patriotic poet, throw himself in the Miluo River, the inhabitants ran to save him. Several boats turned to the water to find him. People handled the oars with strength and rapidity." But in vain. Therefore, the anniversary of Qu Yuan's death was celebrated on the 5th of the 5th lunar month with a boat race. This is only one among several legends. Nevertheless, the *Duanwu jie* is one of the most important traditional festival of China, an occasion for a family reunion. What distinguishes it from others is that people eat *zongzi* and drink wine with a little red arsenic, which is said to fortify the body.

Why *zongzi*? Because people threw *zongzi* in the river after Qu Yuan's death to feed the fishes and to keep the unfound poet's body from being eaten. Red arsenic is toxic and antiseptic, but small doses are not lethal. Some is spread on doors and windows against noxious germs, because according to another legend, the 5th month is a miasma month, and the 5th day in that month is the most dangerous.

As China is populated by 56 ethnic groups, there are many other important **folkloric, ethnic and religious festivals,** such as the Dong "Flourished Cannon" or Firecracker Festival, the Bai 3rd Month Fair, the Yi Torches Festival, the Mongolian Nadam, the Tibetan Xoidun (Yoghourt Festival), the Bathing Festival, the Muslim Bairam (end of fast), the Zhuang Music Festival on the 3rd of the 3rd month, and even several New Year Days a year, according to the calendar adopted by the ethnic groups. Often, on these occasions, young men (girls in matriarchal societies) choose their partners or get married.

Besides the Labour Day, China dedicates a day to recognise groups of persons. So, it celebrates the **International Women's Day,** on March 8 (or *san ba* = 3-8); **Teachers Day**, on September 10; **Youth Day,** on May 4, followed by **Children's Day**, on June 1. Each of these celebrations offers half a day off work and special activities for the relevant group.

To all this must be added a great number of **agricultural festivals** that correspond to different times of the year: the

abundance wish, the spring ox festival, the new rice tasting, the flower picking, the grape festival, the melon festival, the harvest festival, and so on. These festivals are not always occasioned by celebrations, at least in the cities, but a variety of activities correspond to them, such as preparing garlic for the whole year, making sausages and hams, paying homage to the home guardian, etc.

The agricultural (or solar) calendar is very picturesque, with its 24 seasons of 15 days each, based on the four seasons.

But, since 24 times 15 adds up to only 360 days, the use of this calendar requires an adjustment by the addition of an extra month in some years. Thus, in light of all of the above, one may have the impression of only celebrations in this country.

Feeling A Little Less Foreign

When I first arrived here, one needed to have "a reason" to come to China: studies with proof of admission; work with a contract or formal invitation letter; or tourism. But this was not for just anywhere in the country and not for unlimited periods.

Things have changed. It's much easier for tourists to obtain a visa without being "invited" by a friend, relative, or a work unit. Shanghai has already implemented, as an experiment, the three-day visa delivered at entry into the country, and other places such as Hainan, the island province, also admit directly tourists in groups. In December 2001, new policies were adopted to make things easier for business people and investors who have to leave and return many times a year. They may apply for a three-year residence visa. In a few years, foreigners who, as I, live in China and have the intention of continuing to live here, will be able to apply for permanent residence.

But foreigners can't buy or rent an apartment that has not been designated for non-Chinese citizens. Even the Chinese people can't establish themselves unconditionally. There are presently 2 million who hold a temporary residence permit in Beijing alone. With a population over 10 million, the capital can't immediately end the residence registration system; the result would be chaos. However, it's moving prudently toward that, as are the other great cities of the country.

The rents for foreigners' apartments often exceed US$9, 000 a month. Foreign experts in the education or media fields, whose average salary is 4,000 yuan (US$483), can only view them.

Previously, to open a factory, a restaurant or a store, a foreigner had to find a Chinese partner who would act as the owner. The non-Chinese partner could never officially own the majority of the shares, even if in most cases, the total investment came from the foreign partner. More than several people have been cheated by their Chinese partners who, in taking advantage of the situation, ran off with the cash. Since China joined the WTO, a progressive liberalisation is taking place. Foreign entrepreneurs are invited to invest in new fields of activity, such as education, railways, oil, and electricity.

Identity: *Lao wai**

You might have noticed that I myself use the word "foreigner" when talking about the "expats." What seemed strange to me is that some Chinese immigrants in Canada where I was during my holidays once said to me, "You foreigners..." At the beginning, in China, I was mistaken for a Russian as soon as I rode my bicycle, because "it" was. But that day, I had left my bicycle in China...

Another day, a taxi driver in Beijing asked, as they all do, my nationality. I told him to guess. He tried: "British," "German," "American." At the end, I told him I was a Canadian, to which he answered, "*Cha bu duo.*" Well, no, it was not at all "almost the same." Canadians, generally

---

* Word for word: old foreigner. The word "old" doesn't have a negative connotation here. Rather, it should be taken just like "old brother" or "an old friend."

speaking, don't like to be mistaken for Americans, who appropriated for themselves the name of a continent where, combining the three Americas, there are almost two dozens of other countries.

One day, I took a taxi at sunset, and it was raining. After a few minutes of conversation, the driver asked me, "*Ni bu shi ben di ren, dui bu dui?*" (You're not from Beijing, are you?), which he had concluded from my accent. I turned to him. "Me?" pointing to my nose the Chinese way. So, he glanced at me and added, "Ah! from Xinjiang!" I was proud to be taken for a Chinese person, and had used this subterfuge before in Yunnan Province, in order to enter a region where foreigners were not yet allowed to go.

When I go to the Ningxia Hui Autonomous Region, people think I am a Hui woman. In Xinjiang, Uygurs think I am a Kazakh and vice versa. In Beijing Uygur restaurants, waiters and waitresses of this nationality always address me in their language and are all surprised when I reply that I don't understand.

On a flight of Chinese people returning from Canada, my neighbour told me that it was easy to see I was "almost Chinese" because I had been living in China for quite a while.

A Chinese artist whose work I was viewing in an exhibition asked, "*Ni shi bu shi wai guo ren?*" (Are you a foreigner?)

Will I always be another except myself? But, in fact, who am I? China has profoundly changed me, because it arrived in my life at the very moment that I was questioning everything. I first made a *tabula rasa* of my original culture, of my philosophy, of my vision of the world. Then, I examined each element, one by one, choosing in the Chinese culture what I wanted to adopt and, in my former one, what I wanted to keep, and I forged a new culture for myself. It's not integration, assimilation, or imitation, but rather a renaissance.

Sometimes, I think I have 22 Chinese brothers and sisters, because 22 times I've donated blood in Beijing, which now probably runs in the veins of people I will never meet. I also have seven Chinese children, whom I help in finishing their primary school through "Project Hope." These are actions that allow a person to integrate, to penetrate a nation.

Language and Communication

It Was Chinese To Me

Language is a tool of communication, but one may say that, on the contrary, it is sometimes an obstacle to communication, especially in China. When I arrived in this country, I felt as though I was totally illiterate. Even though I had read thousands of books, I had lost all my means and my autonomy. I was obliged to continuously ask, to rely on others.

If I happened to hand my ID card right side up, it's because my photo was on it, because I had no idea of Chinese characters. My Chinese friends laugh when I tell them that, but if I show them a piece of paper with Arabic, Russian, or Greek characters, they understand.

If I bought a pot or a music cassette, a hammer or a pair of boots, glue or thread, I never knew where to go. One of my students often accompanied me, and I thought him very clever, for he always knew which store would sell which article. There were no signs in front of the stores, except "State Store no. 6," which was meaningless to me; I was like a blind person in a library. I could not even distinguish an apartment building from a hospital or an office building.

A decade ago, Beijing seemed so colourless! No show-cases were set up to present attractive merchandise. No attractive colour, no lighting. I remember how struck I was by the "beauty" of Tianjin, which was more advanced than the capital, with its blue mirror frontages, which soon became common in all the construction projects across the whole country. A market economy, marketing, publicity, service to customers, after-sales service, and commercial competition were then unknown. Stores were only big stockrooms for merchandise. Buying something was a burden, as were the consequences, being far from the pleasure that shopping offers today.

At a bus stop, if I asked someone, "Does this bus go to Dongdan?" or "Where should I get off to the Beijing Concert Hall?" people often answered by pointing to Dongdan or Xidan on the bus stop sign. Humiliated, I had to ask again, "Please, tell me the name of the stop." They were astonished, asking themselves whether I was joking, because how could I ask a question in Chinese if I could not read?

Today, still, when I receive a letter in Chinese, I often ask a colleague to read it for me, because I know few characters and can hardly identify them in handwriting. The reaction of those I ask is always to "translate" the letter instead of simply read it out loud, as if the Chinese persons could not divide comprehension and writing.

Communication

Why do most children learn languages much easier than adults? It's because they are not intimidated and they dare to speak. There is no other way to learn a language than to speak it. If a person waits to know all the words and master the grammar, he or she will never speak. Grammar may be studied in manuals, but a language is not made of grammar and vocabulary only. Its main element is communication. In China, this is what is most lacking.

I met Shanghai people who used to go to the Bund every day to practise their English (or French, which used to be very popular) with overseas visitors. They could express their thoughts perfectly, without ever having attended an English class. In the Beijing streets, several school children sing a joyous "Hello!" when they meet a foreigner. But if one asks them a simple question in English, they are lost, and can only laugh shyly. They cannot go any further if they do not hear the exact sentence they had memorised from their textbooks. Young men especially often offer, "May I help you?" but experience has shown me that they can rarely go further. However, at school, they could probably fill the blanks without a mistake. The situation is the same for many English teachers: they know all the language theory, but there is little communication.

Language and Culture

A language is indivisible from a culture and reflects the spirit of those who speak it. According to one's concept of the world, he or she creates a language. For example, in certain African languages, all the colours are classified under three words: green for the earth colour, blue for the sky, and "other colour" for all the rest. In Chinese, the only word *qing* may designate the blue of the sky, the green or the freshness of the grass, or even the black, as was "Lao Zi's ox when crossing Hangu Pass."

In Italian, the same word (*nipotino*) stands for nephew and grandchild, which means that, for the Italians, these two relationships belong to the same category. Also, the Chinese language has different words for big brother and little brother, elder sister, and younger sister, and often calls them accordingly to their rank in the family: second big brother or third little sister, while French has only "brother, sister." English speakers call many persons "uncle" and "aunt", while a Chinese will use a different appellation if the "uncle" belongs to the father's side or the mother's side, if he is older or younger than the interlocutor's parents, if he belongs to the family by blood or by marriage.

Therefore, when studying a foreign language, one must pay attention to the culture that accompanies that language. Why do the Chinese market vendors say "look-a-look," which has nothing to see with English? Because they translate from their own language structure and concept, in which the repetition of a verb indicates a sense of brevity, such as in "give a glance," "sit a little," or "take a bite."

The word "*jia*" means both the family and the house, for the Chinese. Once, I asked a Chinese if he was going back home (*hui jia).* I meant after work. He answered that it was impossible, that his family lived in Hubei Province, and that he would go back to his "house-family" only for Spring Festival. That night, he would go back to his dormitory.

I could continue with many amazing examples, such as to eat medicine, to drink soup, as it is said in Chinese, which are peculiar expressions for the French speaker I am because our mental schemas are different.

We Westerners would like the Chinese not to ask questions about age, marital status, or salary, and not to call a person of a certain age "*lao taitai*" (old lady), but we don't realise our own strange manners when we call a Chinese colleague by his given name or our boss by his family name without a politeness "*lao*" before it. Haven't we noticed that the Chinese don't say "*Wo yao*" (I want) when they address a clerk, if they are polite, but "*Wo xiang mai...*" (I would like to buy...), and that they refuse an invitation to have a cup of tea not by saying "*Bu yao*" (I don't want any), but "Don't disturb yourself" or "I really just had tea"? It would be wise to always observe and analyse the culture that accompanies and nourishes a language that one is learning.

A Wonderful Experience

A Westerner living in China: isn't it a fantastic opportunity? When I remember that Italian manager of a restaurant in Beijing, who crossed off days on his calendar like a prisoner the days of suffering left before his return to his country; he had not understood anything. In fact, he had never tried to communicate with a Chinese person; he had never taken a bus; he had never gone to the market himself.

Some foreigners don't like to be called "*lao wai*"; this is probably because of the word "old." But, to be an old brother, an old friend is not unpleasant! Except in the large cities, where almost every inhabitant has already seen non-Chinese persons, one may expect, when travelling in China, to see people surrounding him or her at the market, checking his or her ability to haggle over prices, judging the competence or seniority in this country by the price he or she pays. Sometimes, they even touch "yellow" hair. In restaurants, they watch to see how expertly the chopsticks are handled.

A journalist asked me recently how I felt when Chinese people look at me and my Chinese husband on the street. I answered, "In fact, I also look at the Sino-foreign couples!" (Don't you?)

Once, I was walking on the street. A cyclist passed me, and seeing a *lao wai*, he turned his head to continue to examine me. There was a truck full of cabbages in front of him and he was going directly to meet it. I made hopeless gestures to him, but in vain. The cabbages didn't complain, but the poor cyclist remained there a few minutes, wiping the blood from his forehead.

What's very pleasant in China are the surprises that fill one's life. Never are two days the same. Here is another of my newcomer's "adventures." I went to a State-owned food store for brown sugar. I had forgotten to ask someone before how to say "brown sugar" in Chinese. At the counter, I ask for *kafei se tang* (coffee-coloured sugar). The shopkeeper gave me white sugar. "No, this colour," I said, pointing to something brown in the store. The girls from the other counters tried to rescue her. One offered sugar cubes for coffee; another one, coffee-flavoured candies. We all laughed, hopeless. I thought that I would return to the university and come back with the correct name. Walking out, I saw something on a shelf in a plastic bag, which could have been brown sugar. "What is this?" – "*Zhe shi hong tang!*" (That is red sugar!), replied the woman, smiling widely. This is what the Chinese call brown sugar! Don't Italians call egg yolk "egg red?" and French "egg yellow"? Don't we call "black tea" in the West the kind the Chinese people call red tea?

*Pinyin** and Translation

Some independent foreign travellers prefer to manage alone instead of relying on an interpreter. Signs in *pinyin* don't necessarily help them. If they haven't studied the pronunciation, would *pinyin* be useful for asking where *Ritan lu* (Temple of the Sun Street) is, or *Zizhu yuan* (Purple Bamboo Park)? Try to pronounce these words using the rules of your language – French, English, or Italian – and you'll see that *pinyin* is almost a foreign language in itself. Moreover, does it help to know how to pronounce *Youyi binguan* (Friendship Hotel), *Pingguo diannao zhongxin* (Macintosh Computer Centre), or *Gongren tiyu chang* (Workers Gymnasium) if you don't know what they mean? As for the logic behind the acronym BJQJDKYD (stands for *Beijing Quanjude Kaoyadian*) and the best one: BJZKATGNJSKYXGS, it's a mystery!

Translating proper names is not always helpful for the foreigners, or even the Chinese people. Imagine that you are a taxi driver in Beijing. You must remember that the Palace Hotel is the *Wangfu Fandian*, the SAS Hotel is the *Huang Jia Da Jiudian*, the Mandarin is the *Xin Dadu*, the Swiss Hotel is the *Gang'Ao Zhongxin*, the Novotel is the *Song He Gongyu*, and the Continental Grand Hotel, the *Wu Zhou Da Jiudian*.

Waiyu = English

Sometimes, as soon as they see a foreign customer coming in, some Chinese clerks call a colleague who speaks *waiyu* (foreign language). Obviously, they mean English. Many

---

* *Pinyin* consists in reproducing with Latin letters the pronunciation of the Chinese words.

Chinese persons have problems remembering that not all foreigners can speak English, and they can hardly imagine that their language is becoming increasingly popular among the non-Chinese population. They often ask us to write down our "English" name. In this case, I always say, with a coy smile, "What can I do; I have only an Italian name?"

On the other hand, their efforts to address foreigners in English are often useless: the restaurants menus are unreadable, and public signs impossible to understand, because they are translated word for word from the dictionary. I often make the Chinese staff notice the mistakes, some of which are very humourous, such as "No burning" for "No smoking," "No flashing" for "No photo taking," and "Washing room" for "Washroom." On invitations or greeting cards, one can still read "the pleasure of your accompany" and "wish you happy" instead of "your company" and "happiness." Some insistently ask me to teach them English or to revise a translation into English, demonstrating that, even though highly motivated, many Chinese persons believe that all the foreigners master English.

When a young girl asked me, in taking my 3 *mao* (0.3 yuan) for the phone call I had just made, why I had spoken Chinese, not English, I answered that, first of all, I was talking to a Chinese person, so I could not speak any English. My "white lie," which left her astonished, was to make her realise that there are other foreign languages than English.

In the wave of opening to the outside world, and even many years before China became a WTO member, some Chinese enterprises and their products often gave themselves an English name. Some of them, when re-translated into English, are totally ridiculous. For instance, Gold Star, which could be simply *Jin Xing* (gold + star) and understandable to foreigners as well, instead has been translated phonetically "*Gao Shi Da*"! Other examples: an advertising company that later declared bankruptcy, had then adopted as its name, for its mellifluous sound, the English word "moron."

Cultural Differences

A Question of Mental Attitude

The long Confucian tradition or what is left of it requires that a person does not announce bad news, does not burden others with negative thoughts, and does not annoy friends with personal problems. What I always deplored, even though I understand it, is that when something is wrong in the foreign expert's way of working or doing, the Chinese counterpart never says a word. The Westerner, used to speaking directly, even roughly sometimes, thinks that if nothing is said, then everything is going well and that people are satisfied with his or her work. However, when one is not "re-invited," as it's called here, that person will be surprised and feel deeply betrayed, especially if he or she has planned to renew the contract and stay longer in China. Upon leaving, the foreign expert will be given a souvenir, be thanked for his or her collaboration and kindly accompanied to the airport, the ticket being paid, but the reason of not being re-invited will remain a mystery.

If good contacts that have been established step by step are to be maintained, people must "desire" the foreign expert's advice, experience, and help. We foreign experts should wait

You
have
done
excellent
work

to discover what is expected from us. Sure, we will notice awkwardness, an enormous waste of time, underuse of material and resources, but we must observe first. A day to suggest changes will come. We must not fall in the trap of accepting the invitation that the Chinese people make for politeness, "Please, give us your advice, help us to improve." We should remain modest and reply that we have so much to learn from them, and wait to be asked many times before making a proposition. I have seen too many foreigners spontaneously answering the invitation saying, "Yes, by the way, I wanted to tell you that you could... you should... it would be better... ". They just put the rope around their necks.

The most difficult for the foreigner to accept is being called "expert" and not be able to act as one. He or she suffers upon seeing things done differently and in a way often "unacceptable" according to Western criteria. The Chinese are a proud nation and this might be overlooked because they are not arrogant or demonstrative but if a Chinese person loses face, an enemy will have been made forever.

We must remember that we are guests in this country. We

have not come to bring civilisation, only a different way of doing things, and not always superior. Steeped in their own culture and resting on the laurels of the alleged superiority of their country as "economically developed," some foreigners forget that there are other ways of thinking and doing in the world. If they consider this thoughtfully, they may avoid deceiving themselves and insulting others.

Beside these fundamental questions that those who want to stay in China for a few years must clarify, not a day passes where little cultural differences and ways of thinking – sometimes diametrically opposed – do not make themselves known. For instance, in their interviews and reports, Chinese journalists often detail the sacrifices undergone to reach his or her aim, such as the ballet dancer who practised so long every

Have a nice trip back home

DU JIN SU

day that her sandals were stained with blood afterward and an artist who worked in a non-heated room for so many years that his hands were deformed by arthritis. A composer fed himself with *fangbian mian* (instant noodles) for months, dedicating himself to his task. The same report filmed in the

West would show the success, the results, instead of the miserable aspects, as though the fact of having suffered made the victory sweeter. Moreover, they consider a man who left his wife and son to help Tibet develop as heroic, even though he didn't visit his family when he heard that his wife was seriously ill; or a mother who abandoned her family to earn money in a large city. These always made me smile, as I think these departures hid a latent divorce. In the West, don't they blame the one who, alleging charity toward the other, neglects his or her family duties?

This different concept between two cultures make the Chinese people appear a little naÔve in our pragmatic eyes, when they quote as indisputable proof the laudatory words of a U.S. president (who probably forgot he did) about an autumn in China – "the most beautiful in the world!" – or a compliment made by another when he did not have the option of remaining silent.

A New Inter-culture

I observe foreigners as much as the Chinese people do, mostly foreigners who have just arrived in the country. A dozen years' experience has led me to the conclusion that the non-Chinese person lacks humility; in other words, they believe in themselves absolutely. For example, a young woman who had arrived to China only six weeks before was invited by her work unit to cover a festival in another province. At the first breakfast, she went to the buffet as everyone had, but came back to the table with four plates, went back again and brought many more, each one containing one portion of a dish. It would have been easy to notice that the others put everything on one plate, and to do the same. She left a negative impression, that of a person who doesn't pay attention to people and facts around her.

Another foreign woman, who had been in Beijing for three years at that time, explained to a newcomer, "When a Chinese invites you to a restaurant, you must pay for both, and if there are many guests, the foreigner must pay his own part of the bill." Instead, I noticed that the Chinese friends are always amazed to see Westerners dividing the amount by the number of guests. Since many foreigners insist, "Let me pay

at least 'my' part!" the Chinese have learned to respect this method to avoid hurting their guests, but find this practice bizarre. It's a vicious circle: as the Chinese people accept it, the foreigners think that the Chinese culture operates the same way. The same has happened in other countries and cultures: the Italian pizza has been borrowed by the United States, who put it back on the market in their Pizza Hut. Clients believe they eat Italian while they swallow an unrecognisable Hawaiian biscuit with ham and pineapple! And Chinese have "invented" for their foreign friends a fruit salad soaking in mayonnaise, as they know the Westerners prepare fruit salads and as the mayonnaise is called in Chinese "salad sauce."

This neo-cultural phenomenon will, I think, extend and intensify around the globe with economic globalisation. And it's a pity, because it's only a cultural bastardisation, a loss of identity, and, eventually, a loss of what gives the exotic flavour in the passage from one country to another, or from one city to another in the same country.

In China, already one can buy souvenirs of all ethnic minorities without leaving the capital city. The southwest batik is sold in Zhejiang; the stone articles of Helan Mountain (Ningxia) can be found in Guangdong; and the Anhui Province ink stones are sold in Shanxi. Also, handicrafts from Russia or Thailand, frontier countries, are now on the national Chinese market. And foreign tourists do not always distinguish Chinese products and others.

Since China started opening to the outside world, less than a quarter of a century ago, all of what comes from other countries is adopted as better and superior, probably because the countries China borrows from have achieved their development before it. Westerners, for their part, have always tended to consider what is different from their own culture as inferior, and to overlook it. Previously, Chinese people were told what to think. Now that China has really opened up, especially economically after its entry in the WTO, the Chinese people are learning to think by themselves and to choose for themselves.

A Few Words on Politeness

China is probably the country (more than any other in the world) with more rites concerning politeness. Let's consider the way of asking the age of a person: one must take into consideration the relation between the two, and the status of the person being asked about with regard to the two former ones. For example, if I ask my neighbour how old her little boy is, I will not use the same form as when I ask my boss the age of his father, or if I address the father himself, or the child himself. Chinese people often ask which sign (zodiacal animal) one was born under instead of the actual age. As each one of the 12 animals occurs every 12 years, it is easy to figure out if a person is 24, 36, 48, or 60 years old.

Americans and Canadians, more than Europeans, are seen by the Chinese as "thank you maniacs." When we discuss this topic with close Chinese friends, they say they feel uncomfortable in front of people who express gratitude for the smallest thing, such as being passed a pair of chopsticks at the table, or having an admission ticket punched at a museum. These acts belong to one's work or to normality; they are not  an expression of generosity, of consideration, or a real service. Are Canadians more polite because they thank the driver when they get on a bus, or the Americans because they say "thank you" (to whom? for what?) stepping onto an elevator, or "excuse me" when they pass someone on the street? Living in the Chinese context, I must say I re-analysed all the politeness reflexes, among other things. I thought deeply about this question and reached the same conclusion as the Chinese, implicit in their behaviour: to thank people for the smallest service puts a distance between people, to show that we have been released from an obligation, that we don't owe anything more, and that we don't consider what the other person has done as natural. It's also saying that we expect to be thanked when we do the same thing.

To be offered money for a service is insulting to a Chinese person. Not that all of them are imbued with generosity; but a service must be repaid with another service, when the time is right. If one spends money for your time and effort, if he or she uses his *guanxi* (relationships) to obtain something for you, you might be ready to be solicited some day to help the person who helped you or one of his acquaintances. If you have "paid" the service received, then you don't owe anything in return, and this is the way Westerners often see things. A Chinese person prefers to create a moral obligation to you or a politeness duty instead of putting in his pocket a few yuan. This is called "establishing *guanxi*." The Chinese are not more or less polite than the Westerners; they are polite in a different way. And those who live in "their" country must understand it.

Furthermore, overseas travellers generally think it is easy to make friends with Chinese people. I think this is an illusion. It's true that the Chinese have only this word on their lips, "foreign friends," for whoever sets foot on Chinese territory, and "dear friends" for TV spectators, etc. But the meaning they give to the word "friend" is not the same as the Westerners'; it's only a polite appellation. Before becoming acquaintances with a Chinese person, one must *eat many kilos of salt together*, as an Italian proverb goes.

Do Chinese people always smile? Are they always happy?

No! They are Confucian and don't bother others with their sorrows and rebuffs. But what a Chinese smile hides, this is another story... Westerners are used to speaking openly, to say directly what they think. In the Chinese culture, this is rough. What is tact for one becomes a lie, hypocrisy, or a swindle for the other. It's not a matter of who is right, but a matter of cultural difference; cultures are not good or bad, just as languages are not good or bad, superior or inferior. The same goes for races and nationalities.

If one asks directions of a Chinese person on the street, and if that person doesn't know, there will be a hesitation in the reply, "*Bu zhidao*" (I don't know), or one might be given the wrong information to hide his or her ignorance. Perhaps the shy answer will be, "*Wo ye bu tai qingchu*" (It's not clear for me either), or even – politeness dictates! – he or she will ask the same question of another passerby, and even going as far as offering to accompany the lost person, especially a foreigner. But try to do the same for a Chinese person who has asked a topographic information of a foreigner (by chance thinking that the foreigner is Chinese), the Chinese person will insist with repeated "*Mei guanxi!*" (no matter, forget it!). And if the foreigner insists on giving an answer, because he or she has lived on that street for years, the Chinese person will stare incredulously, give thanks, and then ask the question of a "real" person, that is, a Chinese person, who may not even know.

Often, Chinese people, always by politeness, refuse to have tea, or a second portion of a dish they adore, or teach their child to refuse candy or a gift. Politeness for us foreigners, at that moment, lies in insisting, because only after two or three refusals will they finally accept. This reminds me bitterly of my childhood: on Sundays, we used to visit an aunt.

My mother always reminded us, before leaving home, that when our aunt offered candies or cookies, to say, "No, thank you!" the first time, but we could accept only if she insisted. Unfortunately, our aunt never insisted. Oh! I would have liked so much to have departed from the rules!

This is the same for the Chinese people when offered a service; they never accept initially and they are the same with each other. For example, a mother-in-law will call her daughter-in-law to tell her that she will be arriving in Beijing on a certain day and specific time; but she will add, "Don't come to the station; the weather is too cold. I'll take a taxi." Woe to the daughter-in-law if she doesn't pick up the old woman! And if she is not prompt enough to tell her mother-in-law that her bed is waiting for her at home, the mother will add, "I'll not disturb you. Some friends will reserve a hotel room for me." Is this hypocritical? Not at all. It is the way to ask without asking, to accept by pretending not to accept.

Maybe the Chinese say "thank you" less often than the Westerners, but instead of the "nice to meet you," they will say to a person to whom they've just been introduced, as they hand over their name cards, "If there is anything I can do for you, don't hesitate to call me." And when their guests leave, they put on their coats and boots and face the winter cold to accompany them to the bus station or until they get a taxi, sometimes paying in advance for their guest, while occasionally in the West, some people close the door when their guests are still on the landing.

To avoid faux pas, to not offend the Chinese hosts, and to avoid confusing situations, a little modesty would be welcome – not to judge, but to observe how the Chinese people think and how they act. In Roma, do as Romans do!

In the Same Basket

If Westerners have a superiority complex, it may be due to the extreme modesty of the Chinese who, always being politeness, even being very proud in their heart of hearts, bow in front of the foreigners, consider them as their masters and as experts, or give the impression of being so, and then, the Westerners believe that they bear the duty of bringing civilisation to this country. It's true, the Chinese people have needed and still need the Western experience in many realms for modernising China, but it must not be forgotten that they themselves are "foreign experts" in other countries. Economically, if China took advantage of loans from the World Bank, it also helped by donating wheat, clothing, blankets, food, munitions, medicine, and money to countries such as Albania, Viet Nam, Democratic People's Republic of Korea, Laos, Cambodia, Tanzania, Congo, Zambia, etc., and have sent them different services (Chinese doctors, for instance, are greatly appreciated in Algeria), teams to build stadiums, railways, dams, etc., and, most important, has cancelled foreign debts of its debtor countries and offered loans again.

Chinese people are not exempt from imperfection compared with other culture. Previously, they were told that China should be brought to the "international standards", but what are they? The danger of generalising, which is not exclusive to them, watches them more than other people. This may be explained by their centuries of remaining closed, when China was satisfied by itself – the Middle Kingdom – and when all that came from elsewhere was rejected, blamed, or not understood. Didn't Emperor Qianlong tell crudely to George Macartney, the special envoy of Britain in 1793, that China had all that was necessary and had no need of foreigners?

In the now-open China, people distinguish what is Chinese and what is not: it's Chinese and non-Chinese. Now, the latter still makes a whole in the collective mind. If, individually, some Chinese persons have travelled around the world and observed the many ways of being, as soon as they are in a group, or publish an article about their sojourn abroad, discuss culture on TV, it's always, "We Chinese" as opposed to "the others, the foreigners." Even when they mention the Japanese, they call them Westerners.

An example: at the beginning of winter, I was wearing a long wool skirt, with high boots and two pairs of stockings. My colleague asked, "You're not cold? For us Chinese, it's not possible..." I made her notice that the distinction was not at this level, that it was not as a foreigner that I was wearing a skirt, but as a person and by individual choice. She didn't seem convinced, and shook her head.

The *Renmin Ribao* (People's Daily) published the article of a Chinese man who'd been to Canada. Mr. Ma summarized the Canadian culture in three points: Canadians don't treat their guests with "alcohol and cigarettes," according to the Chinese saying; they eat mostly cold dishes; and they have no rules in assigning places at table. Let's analyse the content of this article a little. First, the author was talking about a visit he paid to Chinese friends who were newly established in Canada. Should this family be considered as representative of Canadian people? Then, the experience from which he drew his conclusions was a party with more than 20 guests in a small apartment. Undoubtedly, it was not the right occasion to sit around the table or to serve hot dishes. That's why Mr. Ma's conclusions are fundamentally wrong.

Books written by Chinese people who have been living

abroad are very popular in China. Chinese readers want to know! Or they travel themselves, and want to compare their experiences, or they don't have the means to do it, they are curious and fond of information. The first time I read a book of this kind, I destroyed it immediately after finishing it to avoid having it fall into someone else's hands. Fourteen men and women were introducing the "foreign" culture or what they had caught of it (mostly bizarre things) during their three or six months spent in Germany, the United States, or Australia, and almost all of them with a host family. They ended with generalisations such as "the Americans go to bed early," "the Germans pray before meals," or "the Italians spend a great deal of time on the telephone."

In 2001, Christmas didn't pass unnoticed in China. Ambience, decoration, evening meals: everything was present. And the Chinese people participated by wishing each other "Merry Christmas" on the street or at the office. But it's still the United States' culture that dominated. On the whole, the Chinese believe that all the foreigners have a Santa Claus, that they all eat turkey on Christmas Day, etc. When I tell them that we Italians have a meal of fish and sea food the evening of December 24, and that our "*Befana*" (a good sorceress who distributes candies to well-behaved children and coal to those who disobey) comes on January 6, the Epiphany Day, they are all astonished to see that there are other foreign cultures besides the monopoly. Whose fault is it if today's world is an Internet world, and if the Internet expanded over the globe from the United States?

I, for one, never lose an opportunity to remind my Chinese friends and colleagues that each country has its own culture, and that each person is an individual who also has his or her cultural microcosm.

Adaptation – What Confusion!

By wanting to please others and always with a positive intention, it happens that one practises the other's custom, and that both find themselves in an embarrassing situation. For instance, Mr. Xia Lin introduced himself to me, in French, as Mr. Lin Xia but, I, not being aware that he reversed his surname and given name according to the French system, thought that his family name is Xia, while it is his given name.

Or, a Chinese person who lives on the 5th floor (in China, and in Canada as well, the ground floor is the 1st floor) gives his address to a French man, saying 4th floor, thinking as though in France, and the French, believing that the Chinese had calculated the Chinese way, subtracts another floor.

Cultural confusion may cause big problems: when a Chinese person says "next month," he or she means the next page

of the calendar; whether it's the 2nd or the 30th of November, the next month is December, while for many Westerners, next month means "in one month of time." If a Chinese colleague says on Christmas that he is getting married "next year" and that by January 15 he's already married, don't believe that he hastened his wedding date; it's only because of different cultural schemes.

If, on Monday, the first day of the week, a Chinese friend asks if you will be free the next weekend, check the date. He probably meant the weekend of the "next week," while you thought the "coming weekend," which in fact belongs to the current week, so, "this" weekend.

This interpretation of things also creates problems in public transportation. For example, if you ask where to get off for your destination, just after the bus has stopped and the answer is "*xia yi zhan*" (next stop), you may probably remain seated comfortably a few more minutes, because next stop doesn't mean next time the bus will stop, but the following one. For a Chinese, the next stop is "this" stop, as the bus is already moving toward it. The best is to ask another question, because who knows what's in the other person's mind?

Without exact rules, often the context determines the meaning of the words. Numbers, for instance, should deliver very precise information; but in Chinese, they are very vague. A person who is 30+ years old is from 31 to 39 inclusively in China. An appliance costs "some hundreds" of yuan up to 1,000 yuan. A shirt has been paid *yi bai duo* (100+) if it costs between 101 and 199 yuan.

Finally, when translating into Chinese "four times more than last year" or "double of yesterday" subtract one unit and say "*duo san bei*" (three times more) or "*duo yi bei*" (one time more), something that not all translators know.

Studies and Work

Education

When teaching in Canada and later, in China, I often told my students: "At school, you learn how to learn; it's when you leave school that you really begin to learn." After all, isn't there a difference between "studying" how to ride a bicycle and "learning" how to ride it? Unfortunately, too many students are satisfied with their small baggage of knowledge, and once their degree is earned, they don't learn anything else. Today, this situation must change since China's entry in the WTO offers as many wonderful opportunities as challenges and traps. The young ones are those who will benefit more of the former and face the latter and this will not be easy unless they are well-prepared.

Most Chinese teachers and professors who are working now were educated in the "old way." They have risen to their posts without attending Normal School, and if they have a little pedagogy, it is mostly by instinct. Many of them are born of the Cultural Revolution, and are called "the lost generation."

I was always surprised when my Chinese students, between 1991 and 1993, asked me, about a writer I was teaching them, "And what is his style?" They wanted to take notes and learn by rote. They could not understand me when I said that they would discover personally by reading the author's works, and that it was up to them to define the style. They had always been told how to answer exam questions. Personal research was unknown to them; only memorisation had value. I myself had teachers thinking this way, but, in Canada, such a thing was exceptional: a nun who, from being an accountant for the community had become a geometry teacher under the orders of the high authority, could not understand herself the theorems she was teaching us. So, if we had the misfortune to identify the angles of a triangle B, C, and A, instead of A, B, and C, as they were in her manual, she was completely lost.

Often, the Chinese students' M.A. theses are only a synthesis of what others have written on the topic, a collection of outdated articles and wrongly assimilated books. Personal thought is far behind. Still, the Chinese students are creative, but their creativity is latent. How often did the Chinese people marvel at the fact that I "myself" had written the content of my books! I don't see this as a compliment; on the contrary, these words make me blush, thinking that many Chinese books don't follow this pattern.

Students, even at the university level, don't have to write personal works, such as even the primary school children do in the West. They never do any research, and the practice of photocopying has been overtaken by the Internet. It is urgent for them to learn personal thinking. It seems that many people have finally understood that; the challenge rests in how to do it, because their masters themselves are being outpaced by events. Foreigners are often astonished to see how many readers frequent bookstores, some having set up a free reading corner but, compared with the huge population of China, the number of readers and of books per reader has decreased, statistics show. Also, books are being browsed rather than actually read. The current popular topics are technology, international commerce, computers, cartoons, and comics.

Since I've been in China, what's changed more in the education system is that, as it's no longer the government that takes upon itself the university education expenses, students no longer owe the State their four years of studies; previously, they were obliged to accept a State-assigned job and a 5-year contract at the same position – sometimes even longer. Now, graduate students have the right – the obligation – to find a job. They must, as in capitalist countries, highlight their talents and make potential employers pursue them. They must choose what suits them most, discuss the desired salary, and sign a contract that bears favourable social security terms. If they don't respect their obligations, they will be the only ones responsible; their university will have no involvement or save them from an untenable situation.

A second major change in the education system consists in relieving the schoolchildren's tasks. Around 1995, at least in Beijing, homework and exams were eliminated for 1st grade primary schoolchildren, and, from the 2nd grade to the 6th, homework was reduced to one hour a day, and exams were at the end of a term. Special work during weekends, holidays, and summer and winter vacations was prohibited because some children would fall asleep on their notebooks and the parents would finish the work so that their child would not be scolded.

In some cases, parents – not the school – now assign extra exercises or special courses to their children, so that they won't fall behind their comrades, because the entrance examination to advanced levels and in the best schools still exist.

If the child's task is modified, it's of utmost priority to also modify the exam system accordingly. This has not yet been done, which is a huge mistake, indeed. Also, the evaluation of the teachers' competence rests on the students' marks, which is why the latter are overloaded, and why some teachers pass the sponge on copying at the exams.

It's normal for parents to worry about their children wasting time, as they suddenly have leisure hours and are unprepared in how to spend it. The moment has come for the youngsters to complete their learning themselves on topics that they are fond of, in order to develop their creativity, to learn to think about various problems, to involve themselves in the society while taking on responsibilities and helping and participating in activities such as environmental protection. Schools must deepen this research and suggest choices to the children, or it will be reduced to the function of a knowledge vending machine instead of educating the youth for a better society tomorrow. Certainly, the role of the family is not to be neglected, either. Nevertheless, I want to trust democratisation of teaching. There is no reason for this reform to fail.

The third important change that I've witnessed in recent years lies in studying abroad – even children from primary or middle school. Some parents are ready to pay 10 times more than they actually can afford to send their children to renowned schools, which are often associated with a famous university such as Beida (Beijing University) or Qinghua (also spelled Tsinghua). They consider the expense to be an investment in quality. Nothing is too much for their children if they can afford it; even if they have to borrow from the bank, they send their offspring to Australia, Canada, or the United States. Moreover, the tuition fee is so high in some high quality schools in China that several families think that it's better to pay a little more to send their children in a developed country.

Between 1978 and 2001, according to data from the Ministry of Education in October 2001, 320,000 Chinese people had been sent to study abroad by their work units, of which 140,000 have come back. In 1998, 7,300 persons came back from overseas after their studies, five times more than in 1990, and 13,000 are expected to return in 2002, a rise of 13% a year on average. These last years, about 250,000 leave each year, either at the State's expense or on their own. Will they come back? If they use their own money, it's their business, but those who cheat the State's trust in them are very petty, because not only do they appropriate for themselves their own country's public funds, but they become, in most cases, illegal workers in their host countries.

This exodus reveals deficiencies in the Chinese education system. The students who study abroad deprive the State of a fortune that would be useful in the Chinese teaching reforms. It is said that the country loses 4 billion yuan or US$482 million a year this way. If China considers education as an industry and invests in it to develop attractive conditions to its population, not only will it retain enormous funds, but its intellectual elite. However, as China has not yet the means to put its education system at the level of developed countries, it doesn't oppose the education abroad of its citizens, which demonstrates its opening-up policy and its modernisation.

Besides the students, other Chinese persons come back from the States, Europe, Japan, after 10 or 20 years of absence. Some have been leaders in enterprises, specialised technicians, and traders; others have worked in finance, education, scientific research, and some of their inventions have been patented.

Some have always felt guilty for not letting their country benefit from their expertise; others realise that they can live in China as well as abroad. Especially after China's joining the WTO, the market demand has become apparent, and who better than a Chinese person who has lived abroad to serve as a bridge? These persons bring back a precious knowledge, and the Chinese government knows how to appreciate it with concrete means and significant material advantages. The choice of the Chinese people to return to China after a long absence is not easy; China has its own values and life systems, and it is a new emigration for those persons who have to re-adapt themselves to their native country.

Finally, the quality of teaching is increasing but the road is a long one. The teacher is seen as a large pot that pours its contents into little pots. It is extremely difficult to obtain the students' participation in their own education, since they are used to receiving knowledge, not acquiring it. However, at the beginning of this century, people are at least becoming aware – even though many parents and professors fear the consequences – that passivity must make room for the pedagogy of participation, anchored in the real and modern world, a pedagogy of communication.

Education: A Market

What we just said shows that education is a market, which, as everything involving China – because of its huge population – assumes giant proportions. Therefore, China must learn how to maintain it, after having made education its own.

When I first came to China, foreigners who wanted to learn Chinese could choose among only a few institutions, mostly in Beijing. Even those who came to study a specialty such as acupuncture, martial arts, or traditional painting (or the African students who benefited from an exchange programme and came to study architecture or any technology) had to first spend a year at the Language Institute for learning basic language skills, before starting their specialised education. At that moment, the Chinese students' university education was totally cared for by the State.

Year after year, the higher-education institutions were re-

You'll come back after your studies, won't you?

quired to compromise to survive, so they accepted students who had not passed the State admission exams but who could afford the tuition and pension fees. On the other hand, institutions that received foreign students also started to teach the Chinese language, and, a few years later, foreigners were able to study Chinese at almost any university. Presently, 360 universities around the country admit foreign students, from all continents, who study in 200 fields.

In 2001 alone, 50,000 foreign students came to China, raising the total to 350,000. For the first time, their number is about the same as the Chinese students overseas.

Universities have transformed their cafeterias into restaurants, and opened commercial establishments on their campuses for different reasons. First, they planned to industrialise the fruit of scientific research left dormant on the shelves. Second, they wanted to recycle their laid-off workers through the system reform. Finally, they wanted to provide jobs for students who, since 1997, must pay for their studies.

Already in 1993, 5% of the country's students were self-supporting. In Shanghai, it was 38%. The resources from the population allow the institutions to improve the life conditions of their staff, as well as their instruction material.

In 1994, the government asked the already overcrowded universities to cut recruitment by 30%. The number of new admissions passed their economic growth rate by 13.4%. Following this, in 1994-1995, the "tuition fee" system was implemented in 37 universities. The 90,000 recruits had to pay between 1,000 and 2,500 yuan that year, in inverse proportion to their entrance exam scores. The State continued to assure the elite of free tuition.

Many students were taken in by private enterprises, which would hire them later. The real cost of a school year was valued at 8,000-10,000 yuan.

In 1996, half of the country's higher-learning institutions had entered the new system. To allow the poor students to complete their studies, the State injected US$24 million into education. Evening classes and TV teaching became very popular. All kinds of policies appeared, and the terms of getting a loan (grants, in certain cases) were softened. According to the Ministry of Education, 10-20% of the sophomores come from rural families. A great number of their parents have been laid off in the wave of enterprise reform. The government support programme helped thousands and thousands of students around the country.

In 2001, one year of schooling at the university level was estimated to be 6,000-10,000 yuan, excluding board and lodging. At the high school level, the tuition fees were calculated to be 1,200 to 1,700 yuan per year, and for primary school, between 160 and 600. Apparently, kindergarten fees are the highest. According to my empirical information, some parents invest more than 30,000 yuan in their children's primary education, as they want to send them to a "good school."

Also, in 2001, there were 1,000 universities and private colleges around the country, 73 of which were authorised to provide diplomas acknowledged by the Ministry of Education. Of this number, 94 were in the capital city. Private institutions shared 50% of the students with the State establishments.

It's apparent that Chinese students who, at all levels, study abroad and take with them huge amounts that could help improve education inside the nation. More and more foreign institutions also are opening their schools in China and hoard a part of the students and resources; others establish exchange programmes in which the students from both countries receive a part of their education in their own country and the rest abroad. All this shows that the education market represents a large portion of the national budget, and that it is important not to let it escape.

Study: A Human Right

This right – and no less than a right – is one in which China makes sound efforts. Not only does it try to make the 9-year compulsory schooling a reality for the whole country, but it is repairing past oversights by offering comprehensive education (alphabetisation, writing, reading) anywhere it's needed. The national census of 2000 showed that illiteracy had dropped to 6.72% in China from 80% before Liberation (1949).

Presently, the transient population of China include 120 million migrant workers who seek work in urban regions, and their school-aged children number 2.4-3.6 million. They face

three choices: quit school, attend local schools after paying significant extra fees, or attend special schools for migrant children at a much lower cost. Most opt for the third. However, the quality of these schools is not satisfactory. Migrant workers contribute greatly to the cities' development with their labour. Meanwhile, they continue to pay their taxes as rural workers. They bear a double social burden; it would then be logical for their children to have the same right as other children to the compulsory instruction and of the same quality.

The greater the needs, the more the State promotes

instruction. For instance, when I expressed the will to foster a Tibetan child through "Project Hope," the administrators explained that the project covered the whole country, except Tibet, because Tibet has accessible schools for all, and, moreover, if a child wanted to go to school, everything would be provided at no cost: tuition, books, other material, and even food and clothes. When one recalls that before the peaceful liberation of Tibet (1951), 95% of the Tibetans could not read and write, it's remarkable progress!

Also, since university studies are no longer totally taken upon by the State, but must be assumed by the families, new support policies have been implemented, such as grants and loans, so that instruction doesn't become a privilege of the wealthy. Some jobs are also reserved for students.

In June 2001, 170,000 students around the country had already benefited from the State "Help Project," involving 1.26 billion yuan (US$152.3 million).

Employment

If unemployment was almost unknown under the planned economy system, it is because half of the workers were paid without doing anything. What a waste of time, energy, and talent! The market economy wanted to remedy this situation by reforming the State-owned enterprise system. But such a reform could not be achieved without being felt elsewhere – a necessary pain – and this is when efficiency has been chosen over redundancy. Laid-off workers are numerous. A great number have been recycled, others have retired, and the rest are unemployed. However, the government aims at keeping unemployment as low as possible by all means.

Every year, 7 million new workers enter the employment

market. Between 1992 and 1995, at least 100 million farmers quit their sectors to join non-rural sectors, and the urban population is now 30% in China.

Since the students no longer study at the State's expense, studies and work have been divided into two independent fields.

The freedom to find a job means competition, obviously, and competition is based on qualification. That's why many young workers return to study as soon as they have saved a little money, to improve their future. Presently, the MBA (Masters in Business Administration) and the MPA (Masters in Public Administration) are very popular. Since they lack experience because they are young, and because the older ones belong to another time, the candidates for jobs must increase their competence. This is necessary, especially in the non-governmental enterprises, the private enterprises that are financed by mixed funds or totally foreign funds.

In seeking work, young people don't ask their parents' advice anymore nor do they follow their friends' advice. They pay attention to their own interests. One youngster out of four, accordingl to the Beijing survey on youth in 2000-2001, has changed work once or more often, mostly by transfer, but also by their own decision, aiming for better pay. Half of the young who responded to the survey said that they worry about their future, 8.8% say they are troubled by the stress of unemployment, and 40.7% say they think about it occasionally. The degree of concern is in inverse ratio to the level of education.

For the staff already in the State units, competence is not always the criterion when the reform requires the laying-off of workers, because other criteria (age, rank, title) can't be overlooked without resulting in social upheaval.

The fields offering the most postings at present are information technology, administration, and foreign languages. The new employment style is called "mutual choice" (employer-employee). The country has oriented itself on gain, henceforth, and each one takes part in the race for money. Succeeding means making lots of money.

Hundreds of workers prefer not to sign a contract and to keep their options open, in case a better opportunity comes along. Also, the workers rotate and their mobility is staggering. The risk is high for enterprises that pay to train the staff, because some quit as soon as they have just become productive.

The service sector is still the weakest in China. The loopholes are obvious in administration, and the study of consumer trends, marketing, and publicity are still uncharted territories. Especially after entering the WTO and along with its modernisation, China needs new competencies and new qualifications. It must, therefore, extend specialized education. It's more than words to say in this country that the future belongs to the youth.

China in Motion

Remarkable Changes

Parents don't notice that their child grows a little each day; but their friends who see the same child three or four times a year are surprised by the changes. The situation is the same for me with China. When my friends and relatives visit, they exclaim in surprise what has changed since their last visit, and I'm aware of the continuous evolution. By remarkable changes, I mean "appreciable" as well as "can't not be

noticed." The range of examples is enormous.

Let's first discuss food, because many phenomena are related to it. Not even a decade ago, ration coupons went out of circulation. Previously, people needed them to buy oil, eggs, and meat. During my three-month stay in Beijing in 1989, I couldn't buy cookies because I didn't have coupons. In 1991, my students sometimes offered me coupons that they wouldn't use to buy rice because they couldn't cook in their dormitory, but I, not being a resident, should have paid more without these pieces of paper. Nowadays, China has almost abolished poverty, in accord with its development planning policies. Production and distribution of food are ensured in the country and so coupons have fallen into disuse.

Also, I have observed the birth and the growth of fast food in China. The first McDonald's opened in Beijing in April 1992; today, it is difficult not to see a McDonald's in any direction. In the same fast-food wave were Pizza Hut, Domino's, Dunkin' Donuts (which went bankrupt after a few years), A&W, etc., including all the foreign ice cream products, such as Wall's, Nestlè, and Bud's that are the most successful. To this can be added cold meats, such as cooked ham, salami, sausage, prosciutto, etc., candies, fruit juices, Starbuck coffee shops – all that can be eaten or drunk and almost in an unlimited stream – after China's entry in the WTO.

However, "fast food" doesn't necessarily mean foreign. A type of Chinese fast food develops alongside the Western style, not to mention the millions of hot meals served directly from the pan to the work units' canteens all around the country – in the universities and on the street. For instance, the KFC model gave birth to the Shanghai Ronghua chicken. There are also vegetarian fast food chains; others are based on tofu only.

Urbanisation imposed changes even to the food culture. The night markets along the streets, where each stall sold only one product, mostly specialties from various regions of the country, have now become covered food markets, which are open from morning to evening. In a former railway station, for example, each counter has a station bearing the name of a culinary region or a province of the country, and sells only its specialties. These fast-food markets can be found at Wangfujing, a famous shopping street in Beijing. For hygienic reasons and because of urbanisation also, vendors of roasted chestnuts, flat cakes, hawthorn brochettes, mutton meat

brochettes, pineapple or melon pieces on a stick, thin pancakes folded in nine (called *jianbing guozi*) are no longer visible on the streets. Buying and eating these little marvels indoors lacks its former charm; also, if we don't see them, it doesn't occur to us to eat them. For these attractive products

– for tourists and locals – a demise is sadly guaranteed.

The brochettes of caramelised hawthorns can be found in supermarkets, covered by an aluminum bag, at the frozen food counter. The same can be said for many specialties that were previously reserved for certain days or festivals of the year, such as the *jiaozi* or the *yuan xiao* (see the section above on the Spring Festival), which can now be eaten year round. But this reduces them to the rank of ordinary dishes.

Development has brought on the market on each corner the country fruit and vegetables from everywhere. We can find Hainan coconuts in Inner Mongolia as well as Xinjiang *hami* (a place) melons in Jiangsu Province. The choice of fruits and vegetables is not only more extensive, but the limits once imposed by the seasons no longer exists, and strawberries and watermelons can be found in January as well as in May, which is a pity. Certain imported products, such as the Ecuadorian bananas, have chased national products out of the market, or cannot compete with them, according to my palate, which prefers the domestic treats. Foreign food has entered China, too, and not only the great hotels' restaurants. In large cities, more choices are being offered.

Finally, the Chinese people's diet has changed, and not always for the better. If, some time ago, the diet was imbalanced due to poverty, today it is due to overabundance. Rice, which has long been a staple, has already disappeared at the tables of the wealthy. Moreover, meat consumption is far too high in the ordinary diet, and obesity has become a new problem for the Chinese people, especially the young. Not only is obesity a problem in itself (aesthetically, in terms of functioning and decreased efficiency at work), it causes many other ailments, which are on the increase in Chinese society, such as heart disease and high blood pressure.

It's said that the Chinese population eats better than before, and that the young are taller and more developed than the previous generation. That means that they consume more protein, but often at the sake of fruits and vegetables. They eat more meat, but fatty meat. Milk is being distributed in schools – in Shanghai and Beijing initially. Fresh cow milk has replaced soy milk at breakfast, without regard about the animal fat.

Summer camps for "re-shaping" chubby children have become a social necessity. Presently, there are 70 million overweight persons in the country, and 27% of the children under 15 are in this situation. Obesity of urban boys has risen in five years from 6.7% to 10.7% in 2000.

The number of diabetic persons grows by 3,000 a day in China! One hundred million Chinese people suffer from high blood pressure, and their rate rises by 2.5% a year. Linked to stress and lack of physical exercise, high blood pressure threatens the new generation especially, the one that works under great stress and at a very different rhythm compared with their parents' generation. Nevertheless, several social organisations are conscious that health should not be estimated only by the layer of fat; people have a better chance of getting information to establish a good, balanced diet. Playing sports is also greatly encouraged.

On the other hand, one can't help but notice the waste of food, in family homes as well as in restaurants. The virtue of economy doesn't enjoy the rank it used to in the Chinese culture.

This leads to another change: **consumption**. The Chinese dream has changed. Where previously one considered pursuing higher education as a way to a prestigious position and to be useful to society, now people think of earning a great deal to be able to spend a great deal. Success means having money. All conversations include the eternal "*duoshao qian?*" (how much?). If a neighbour or a relative buys an apartment, a cellular phone, a microwave, or a new brand of cigarettes, the first question is always, "How much did you pay?" Buying has become the primary hobby of many – I don't say most – Chinese people.

To own a car is the dream, admitted or not, of half the population, and not just any kind of car, even though only 2% of Chinese households can afford it. To be the owner of a house once provided by the work unit is no longer enough; a new (large and comfortable) house is seen as requisite. This desire is praiseworthy, since a pleasant environment is one determinant of the quality of life. But some – too many, unfortunately – fill their new houses with furniture, appliances, and odd tchotchkes to display their wealth, with a glaring lack of taste and judgment.

On a smaller scale, can a grandfather pick up his grandson at school without buying a treat or a toy on the way back? Is a walk with the family on Sunday possible without buying a grilled sausage, cotton candy, a balloon, a Coca-Cola, a T-shirt, or a new gadget for children or adults?

Yet another significant change that I noticed lies in the development of **transit and communication**. When many persons own cars, taxis are no longer a privilege of wealthy foreigners. Some workers treat themselves to a taxi ride to work. The urban and inter-urban road network has greatly improved – with new streets, the widening and repair of old ones, new highways, better designed interchanges, computerised traffic control, increased police intervention, and more comprehensive traffic lights. Two other cities after the capital and Tianjin now have subways: Shanghai and Guangzhou.

Railways have increased in length and speed. Computerisation of ticket sales has greatly alleviated the tiresome situation, even though there is still much to achieve in the railway field.

What can I say about **information**? Newspapers that were read before only in the public *baolan* (community board) have proliferated, and the number of their readers, who either subscribe or buy at the stand, has increased accordingly. The papers' contents are more open, varied, and democratic; their printing quality, including colour, photos and cartoons, puts them at the level of the well-known international dailies. The same can be said for Chinese magazines, not to mention the huge number of foreign magazines in the original languages or in Chinese translations, which are distributed around the country.

Television broadcasts are aired through a multitude of local, provincial and regional stations, and international channels (United States, Japan, Russia, etc.). The China Central Television now has 10 channels, one being exclusively English and broadcast 24 hours a day. But the most important in such an evolution is the content. Today, the Chinese media provide information in many fields that were forgotten, ignored, or hidden before, and this information is appreciated for its quantity and its quality.

The Internet, which was at the dinosaur stage a decade ago, has achieved exponential progress, while the telephone network has not reached its peak. With the residential telephone network expanding all over the country, individuals have graduated from beepers to mobile telephones with always more sophisticated accessories, from photocopy machines to e-mail, from long distance calls made from the post office to overseas calls made from anywhere with a phone card. Not long ago, in order to use a telephone, one had to line up, often outside, in the cold and, when communication was established, breakdowns were frequent or the reception was inaudible. Only a decade ago, one still had to complete an application and wait for years before the telephone could be installed in the home. From practically nothing 20 years ago, the fixed and mobile telephone subscribers reached 110 and 43.24 million in 1999 respectively, or 13% of the country's total population, and 28.4% or the urban population.

Today, what child has not yet put his or her fingers on a computer keyboard? I for one heard the word "Internet" for the first time in 1993. I asked right and left what "that" was, and I could not get a satisfactory answer. Nevertheless, in 1998, China already had 2.1 million Internet users, 4 million in 1999, 8.9 million in July 2000, and 45.8 million in June 2002 – estimated to reach 200 million in 2005.

Moral Values

Finally, what about the moral values of China? If, nowadays, the blame for all ills no longer rests on the depraved capitalists who spread their so-called virtue in the Middle Kingdom, who's responsible for the loss of the values that have prevailed for millennia and guided the Chinese nation? The deified economic progress certainly has something to do with it, as well as the unbridled competition that places profit above all. The Cultural Revolution left a chasm in the culture, and material aspirations are filling it in. Certainly, the evolution of moral values has been obsessed with economic development.

The Confucian principle of "love others" left its place to seek monetary opportunities. The pursuit of fortune and happiness (or pleasure) has created a god of hedonism, a deity to which the following has been sacrificed: tolerance, frugality, and modesty, in other words, the traditional virtues of the Chinese people. The lack of moral values has tarnished China's international image.

When the whole country was poor, desires were virtually unknown. Then the motto of "get rich" was launched, but without guiding the nation to a better way of living. Now that a trench has been dug and that the gap between those who have and those who don't keeps widening, the latter of these groups have desires and they take, by any means. Besides corruption, which is pervasive at all levels, another great social harm exists among those who have manage wealth. For example, if the State needs land for civil construction, a good amount will be paid, one that should be shared among the farmers who have to move but often they never see the money, while the local authorities hold banquets, offer lavish gifts, buy cars, or travel abroad. How can such persons sleep peacefully every night?

It is important that traditional values (for instance, Chinese modesty, which consists of remaining in the background) balance the new values that are needed in a modern world, such as showcasing one's personality and talents.

Fortunately, the country's leaders are aware of this and are working to re-establish a true, concrete, and practical socialist ethic. In 2001, two very important events contributed, I think, to accelerate the edification of a moral code supporting the social morality of China: the entry of China in the WTO and Beijing's victory as the host of the 2008 Olympic Games. To govern a country with 20% of the global population is not safe and easy. A small mistake can turn into a monumental blunder. Maintaining the current pace of development while accelerating social progress means overall to establish a social welfare system; develop education based on science; accelerate the opening up; pursue the reform of agriculture, industry, and State-owned enterprises; stimulate national demand; finish the Three Gorges project; fight corruption, drugs, and AIDS; attract foreign investment; be an active WTO member; prepare for the 2008 Olympic Games; develop the western part of China; improve the living conditions of the whole nation, etc. – what other country has so much on its plate?

Habits on the Decline

Bad habits fade as a matter of course, generally. For instance, Chinese people often ask foreigners their age or ask among themselves, thinking that the foreigners don't understand. But they have become more discreet or at least more aware, if not totally convinced, that matters of privacy for Westerners requires discretion among the Chinese people in turn.

I will talk here about good habits that, following the opening up, are dramatically decreasing, and will soon disappear. The first ones concern **health**.

When I first came to China, in scorching heat, I was served hot tea everywhere. Used to cold beverages to refresh myself, I was surprised, but experience soon taught me that heating the inside of the body balances the temperature and helps to mediate the external heat. In Harbin, a city northeast of China, inhabitants eat ice cream in the winter for the same reason. Another reason why the Chinese people did not drink cold beverages was to avoid shocking the body's system. There is nothing like a cold bucket of water to revive a person who's fainted. The cold shocks a warm body; muscles and internal organs contract initially and then slowly begin to function again. Since each household today has a refrigerator, people are forgetting this wise principle.

One of the most striking images of China for foreign tourists was to see the Chinese people rise early, even before sunrise, and practise *taiji* (martial art), *qigong* (a vital circulation technique), rhythmic exercises, or aerobic dancing everywhere: in parks, on public squares, on university campuses, or on the grounds behind a factory or an office. However, the modern, fast life has forced this healthy morning practice to somehow become lost in the shuffle.

When they waited for a bus, read newspapers, or played cards on the sidewalk, Chinese people used to squat. This position is very comfortable, allows the body to rest, and is good for the digestive system. However, besides the fact that modern and elegant clothes don't allow this position to prove its merits, it's a matter of education. Confucius outlined the principles of how a civilised person should stand tall like a pine tree, sit like a bell, lie on the bed like a bow, and walk like the wind (*li ru song, zuo ru zhong, wo ru gong, xing ru feng*).

Chinese people were also used to **punctuality**. It was considered better to wait than make others wait for you. When I came to China with a tourist group, in 1985, if one of us had not boarded the bus at 8:00 exactly, the appointed time for departure, our Chinese guides believed something bad had happened and alerted the whole hotel staff, sending them to find out what had happened to our tardy companion. But, now, not only do they go to bed much later than before and have difficulty getting up early, they always have the *du che* (traffic jam) excuse, a situation that didn't exist before, when only bicycles circulated in the streets.

Also well, finances permitting, people are more inclined to jump into a taxi than to ride their bikes; bicycles are also being regarded as a public nuisance in cities. Shanghai and Beijing are doing all they can to improve the situation for motor vehicle circulation, and the poor bicycle doesn't have the right of way anymore.

What's also disappeared is the appellation *Tongzhi* or "Comrade" in addressing a colleague as well as the restaurant waitress, the shoemaker, or a passerby on the street. It is not a judgment of good or bad; this change, as well as the following one, indicates the evolution of society and of human thought.

If it was indecent to show one's feelings, the Chinese people have always been less discreet when having a physical examination in front of other patients; in going to the bathroom, without closing the door where there is one; or going to public showers. All of this makes most Westerners feel shy. On the other hand, we Westerners are used to tender words and affectionate displays even in public, while old Chinese couples used to call each other "Comrade" until their deaths. Only recently have lovers become visible. They began by holding hands, then sitting closer to each other on park benches, then pecking with increasing ardour, to the point of annoying those close enough to witness their passionate expressions.

In another matter, a celebration without **firecrackers** is not a celebration for the Chinese population. Firecrackers were prohibited in Beijing on September 1, 1993. Previously, at the first opportunity, they would be lit by the thousands on campuses, in the streets, courtyards, and parks. At the most intense moments, it was impossible to hear the radio or the TV because the air was saturated with noise (and smoke),

and for several days, shredded red paper strewed the grounds. Sweeping it away would have been like sweeping away happiness.

There are a huge variety of firecrackers. Some are small, with a fuse linked with a thread and are sold in batches of 100 or 500. People hang them on trees or at the end of a stick. There are also small bombs that explode at once, which can be startling, and also boxes of 16 big firecrackers that light in sequence once the first is lit; usually someone lights it and then places the package on the ground before running off.

These are the most deafening. Also, flares sizzle high in the sky, shooting glitter along their paths; others zigzag like spermatozoa seeking the celestial ova. Others fly like arrows, bursting with noise and colour. From a 50 cm paper tube, we can watch dozens of blooms – some very nice; others, subtle – but one every second. There are also flying spirals, like fluorescent snakes and cylindrical boxes like big sausages from which thousands of sparkling, brilliant stars shoot in all directions. When all this explodes at the same time, the evening sky is as clear as day.

Even after the prohibition, people started to light firecrackers, and infractions have increased yearly since. In Beijing, during Spring Festival week, from February 12 to 18, 2002, almost 300 persons were hurt, of which 100 were children between the ages of 4 and 10, and 224 fires required firemen intervention, compared with 51 during the same period in 2001.

Firecrackers are so intrinsic in the Chinese soul that the authorities have been obliged to make concessions. It was impossible to destroy this huge part of the national culture, a manifestation of joy and life, and important element of family gatherings.

However, because of the great number of accidents, some of which have been fatal, the control is tighter on the production and sale of these products, and those that don't conform to the standards are seized and destroyed. In 2002, 100,000 policemen and volunteers patrolled the streets in the capital on the lunar New Year's Eve to enforce this.

Some adequate and supervised places are designated for firecrackers lighting, and experienced pyrotechnicians handle them, but to prevent people using firecrackers and fireworks just anywhere in the urban areas, more supervised places should be designated so that the people would not have to travel far from their homes.

New Concepts

The Holiday Economy

Since 1999, National Day has given everyone a whole week off, including a regular weekend – two days that are "paid back" by working a Saturday and a Sunday before or after the holiday but three days are given "free." In 2000, this long holiday included the Spring Festival and Labour Day, May 1.

The original and exclusively Chinese measure called the "holiday economy" has boosted the national economy by stirring up many opportunities for money to circulate. The number of national tourists – 28 million in October 1999 almost doubled in October 2000 to 55 million, and then 63.97 million in 2001, while the tourism global revenue went from 14.1 billion* yuan to 22 billion in 2000 and 24.98 billion in 2001. The three seven-day holidays of 2001 totalled 200 million trips, and collective expenses of more than 70 billion yuan (US$8.46 billion).

The experiment succeeded; China can be proud of it, and this model could be followed by countries where the economy is stagnant. Since the beginning of this week-long holiday, in

---

* 14,100,000,000. Billion is used with the American meaning; 10^9.

May, in October, and in February, the rhythm of life and work of the Chinese people has changed. The year is conceived in three periods of respectively three, four, and five months, divided by holidays that they start dreaming of as soon as one holiday period has passed. People developed a taste for it and felt deprived by not being able to enjoy it at the beginning of 2002, when Friday, the 4th, a work day, interrupted the January 1, 2, 3 holiday, which could have extended over the weekend to Monday morning, "for boosting the national economy," as the people claimed.

The Chinese households' savings passed 7 trillion yuan, an enormous consumption power. The holiday economy phenomenon shows that the improved living level has deeply changed the concept of consumption. The traditional demand for basic goods has allowed room for leisure, comfort, and development, while the holiday economy, besides providing a rest for workers, stimulates the consumption of varied products, such as those of culture and of the tourism industry: hotel trade, restoration, transportation, entertainment, and historic.

A passing phenomenon? It remains to be seen. Meanwhile, it's fruitful. Such a concept doesn't exist in the West. On the contrary, many stores close during holidays. People spend their holidays near the sea, leave the country, or go camping. Consumption during holidays vary more in quality than in quantity. In China, people flow into the cities. With time, the concentrated holiday economy will probably disappear and be replaced by activities and leisure holidays.

Travelling for Pleasure

The three long annual holidays have ingrained an already

established tendency: to travel instead of going to the hometown for family holidays. Not only did revenue rise after the 40-hour week on May 1, 1995, the Chinese people enjoy more free time and tourism gained fans. Since the people of China graduated from meeting the basic needs, such as clothing and food, they now are free to focus on raising their quality of living and culture by tourism. One survey shows that family expenses for tourism is 10% of the budget in Beijing and 11% in Shanghai.

Tourist destinations as well as the kinds of travelling change with the fact that more people travel with their own car, and that more persons travel independently (at their own

expense, not with subsidies from their work units). Many Chinese no longer choose popular sites (Huangshan Mountain in Anhui Province or the Xi'an terracotta army) as their destinations but opt for the west of the country or natural sites. In recent years, the State has promoted places such as the

Ningxia Hui Autonomous Region, and hordes of people go there. Hainan, the island-province, with its wonderful beaches, is a new destination, as well as Yabuli with its skiing and other winter sports and activities. The Special Administration Regions of Hong Kong and Macao also host a high number of tourists from the mainland.

Time and finances permitting, more Chinese treat themselves to holidays abroad. There were 2.93 million such travellers in 1992, 4.71 million in 1995, and 5.32 million in 1997. In 2000, at least 10 million Chinese citizens went abroad for tourism, and their total expenses passed US$10 billion*.

Southeast and Pacific Asian countries are the top destinations, but the Chinese people also go to the United States and Russia. After New Zealand, Malaysia, Thailand, Philippines, Indonesia, Laos, Nepal, Republic of Korea, Japan, Viet Nam, Myanmar, Cambodia, Brunei, Australia and the two Chinese Special Administrative Regions of Hong Kong and Macao, five other countries – South Africa, Germany, Egypt, Turkey, and Malta – have been added to the list of desired destinations for the Chinese citizens who travel at their own expense; these are countries with which China has made arrangements to facilitate travel.

Also, the Chinese economy continues to develop steadily. The yuan remains stable, while other Asian currencies have been devalued, allowing the Chinese to travel with their personal savings. In 2001, the urban population revenue per capita increased by 8.2%; the farmers' revenue, by 4%. Savings of the two groups reached a record of 7 trillion yuan, an increase of 800 billion since the beginning of 2001. Beijing and Guangzhou's GDP per capita reached US$3,000 in 2001, and

---

* 10,000,000,000.

Shanghai's, US$4,000, the highest in the country after Hong Kong, Macao, and Taiwan. Shanghai reached the rank of countries and regions with middle or superior revenue.

Getting a passport for a Chinese citizen is now easier. Since the end of 2001, some restrictions have been lifted. The validity period on visas for Hong Kong and Macao has been extended; the requirement for invitation letters from the destination country and exit registration cards issued with passports have been eliminated; special entrance corridors for Chinese citizens have opened in 10 large cities; and, finally, by the end of 2005, citizens from large and medium cities will be able to apply for a passport by presenting only their residence registration card (*hukou*) and their ID card.

However, even though 10 million travellers go abroad every year, the number accounts for only 1% of the country's population. It is therefore easy to understand why the reproductions of world-renowned monuments and sites, in places like Beijing World Park, hold such an attraction for the other 99% of the people.

During the 40 days before and after Spring Festival each year, travelling becomes a nightmare, but a necessary nightmare, tradition obliging! These 70 million migrants who came to the cities try to return home to spend the holiday with their families. Workers hired in positions away from their native place and students all go back to their families. In 2002, between January 28 and March 8, about 1.74 billion travellers took trips, 100 million more than in 2001. From February 7-9, 3.6 million persons took a train in the country. February 18-20 saw another peak of 4.1 million persons returning to work or university. Between 1996 and 2000, China built 240,000 kilometres of roads, of which many are high quality. In 2002, 4% more travellers than the year before took the bus.

Millions will spend hours or days on trains after having lined up from 6:00, for several days, in order to buy a ticket. Others will need to detour or complete their trip with several stops (from A to B, B to C; C to the final destination D) to reach home, their arms overloaded with gifts for their family. Rural women, with babies strapped on their backs, will cover thousands of kilometres to be with their husbands who work in the city and to be on time for Spring Festival. Because the Chinese people are family-oriented, it's de rigueur for them to spend festivals with their family members. Since it is still impossible to buy a return ticket, the "pleasure" of finding a ticket to go back will start a few days after arriving.

Merging May Be A Solution

Since the beginning of enterprise reform and of education reform, the concept of mergers has been implemented in both areas, and this phenomenon has been witnessed more often, even in universities, allowing the enterprises to reduce their expenses and raise their quality. For example, take the Academy of Social Sciences of China, with its world-renowned scientists. In 2001, the ASSC incorporated several research institutes and revised the recruitment process, wage negotiations, system of rewards, scientific research, and property rights; formed a scientists' team and relief team; planned downsizing from 80,000 to 20,000 by 2005; and outlined risk investments in institutes and joint ventures, etc. The government encourages money-losing ventures to merge, and after China's entry in the WTO, invites foreign enterprises to merge with Chinese enterprises. A recent case was the one of Danone, a food producer in France, which absorbed Wahaha of China.

Bank Loans

Credit was once considered immoral. The first credit card owners used it discreetly. In fact, China mostly advocated debit cards. Now, banks allow loans for various purchases: real estate, car, education, and even travel. A January 2002 survey in 57 Chinese cities revealed that 29% of those who seriously consider buying a car would do so with a bank loan.

Loans to students are still flagging, because on what basis should the lending institution trust a young person who has no financial resources and no employment? The State guarantees part of the loan, but who makes up the rest in case of default? It's risky, which is why, when I was a student in

Canada, this kind of loan was on the "honour system," an initiative of a non-government society. Now, the provincial government guarantees the education loans made by the banks. If the student defaults on the loan at the end of his or her studies, the student is subject to his or her wages being

garnished.

Insurance

Another financial service has established itself in the Chinese economy, particularly in the wave of the enterprise reform. If the enterprise is relieved of health care and old age pension, and if unemployment results from laying off redundant workers or from closing enterprises operating at a loss, someone has to assume these expenses, and it is the individual, which is why the need has arisen for personal insurance.

A concrete example: since the beginning of 2002, a person who works in a State unit must assume the first 2,000 yuan of medical fees (the deductible); half of the rest will be refunded. From the moment of retirement to the age of 70, the non-refundable portion will be 1,500 yuan, and the refund,

60%. After 70, 70% of the fees will be refunded. Before this reform, the same work unit allowed a monthly allocation of 60 yuan to each worker to cover potential medical expenses. If the employee spent more than 720 yuan, 85% or 90% of the surplus, according to seniority and status, were refunded at the end of the year.

As a foreigner, my situation is different. Chinese people are not well-informed and believe that we foreigners are granted every service free of charge. Let's say I undergo a routine gynaecological examination. I may go to the hospital assigned by my work unit, pay 200 yuan for what is called a "registration fee" (in fact, a non-refundable consultation fee), and the visit will cost 348 yuan, which is refundable. If I choose to go to a hospital for Chinese patients, where I will pay a 40-yuan "registration fee" (5 for Chinese citizens) and 84 for the examination, but my work unit will not refund me any of that. We will both come out ahead in such a situation.

The advantage of the first hospital? Doctors speak English and most have been trained abroad. They receive only one patient at a time, and we foreigners may close the door if we want a private consultation. Another advantage: we reportedly line up for less time, but I waited for over two hours on my last visit.

Before becoming a WTO member, China made promises to foreign insurance companies. Territory limitations, limits concerning services provided, a commercial or personal presence, kinds of enterprise, and protection of property – all have been planned for the next three, five, or ten years, and limitations will decrease. Concerning operations, first China will allow insurance companies to provide their general insurance services to overseas enterprises, and, second, property insurance to foreign-funded enterprises in China and related services such as liability insurance and credit insurance the second year, and, finally, the whole of their general insurance services to Chinese and foreign customers. Health insurance will follow in kind.

Currently, the Chinese Commission for Insurance Regulation is eliminating laws and rules that conflict with the WTO rules. New rules are being outlined, and the insurance system is under reform. Meanwhile, qualified staff is being trained.

These new measures will allow the Chinese insurance sector to face the WTO challenge. One can therefore be anxious about the enormity of the potential market, which will open to the outside world in this field, a market presently flourishing in China and largely coveted by foreign insurance companies, which possess both funds and experience.

Olympic Spirit

How could I not mention the Olympic fervour that has been exciting the nation for eight years? For the first time in my life I have observed a nation taking an active, enthusiastic part in the bid for the organisation of the 2000 Olympic Games first, and then, after the failure, beginning a new march toward the second attempt – successful this time – with the almost unanimous support of the nation and for the joy not only of the capital's citizens, but of the whole country and even many other countries of the world.

As I contributed greatly to the translation of the Beijing bid for the Olympics, I consider the capital's success a personal achievement, and in July 2001, while I was in Canada, tears of joy replaced my tears of sadness over the former bid.

The Olympic spirit has become a value in itself for the Chinese people. The masses followed the news avidly on this topic; not only do they have an interest in sports and physical exercise, but for reports on former Games, on international star athletes, and on the progress of national athletes. The 21st Universiades (university student games) held in Beijing shortly after the proclamation of the capital's victory for the 2008 Games generated a special enthusiasm, as well as the soccer World Cup that, for the first time, has seen China qualifying for the finals.

Organising the Olympic Games is not just an honour. Preparation involves urgent and weighty responsibilities, which Beijing has promised to achieve in time: develop clean energy, control industrial pollution, and move 200 polluting enterprises beyond the Fourth Ring Road, achieve 40% of green coverage in the capital, etc.

The awareness of environmental issues and responsibility for each citizen to protect it were born in the wave of the Olympic spirit. This idea has taken root deep in the youngsters' minds: they plant trees and take care of them; nurse wounded animals; clean sites such as the Great Wall and riverbanks; save water and electricity; recycle paper, plastic, and glass; collect used batteries and throw them in designated safe places where they can be destroyed without damaging the environment; or take lost animals to organisations that will place them back in their natural environment. All of these are practised by the children, who encourage their families to do likewise. At the national level, the government protects endangered species, especially the Tibetan antelope, giant panda, white-headed eagle, various types of tigers, and the golden monkey.

Law

Shortly after China's opening to the outside world in 1978, Westerners started to negotiate projects with the Chinese. They were often disconcerted by the "slow motion" negotiations. The Chinese people found these foreigners very indelicate because they, upon first sight, spouted on about rights and duties, and of signing contracts. Now, both sides are better informed on the functioning rules of the other side, and this helps to prevent difficulty and misunderstandings.

Today, what is law in the life of the Chinese citizens is another example of China's development. Take contracts, for

example. In 1993, a Shanxi Province publisher agreed to publish my illustrated haiku collection. When he saw me hesitate, he offered a contract; all the blanks remained empty, except for the book's title. No publication date, no number of copies to be printed, no royalty percentage. All this would be discussed later. Two years later, I found a gallery to hold my first painting exhibition in China. After discussion, the owner told his assistant, "With foreigners, we have to sign a contract." She took a sheet of paper on which she wrote by hand, "Dear Lisa, Our gallery will hold an exhibition for you on January 7, 1995." I had been teaching for two years at the Foreign Language University without ever seeing a contract. When I changed positions over to the Central Television, after one year of work, I had to remind the relevant person every year that we had to renew my contract, which was often done in the middle of the following year. It was not negligence, but a different concept.

For the Chinese person, a piece of paper is just that: a piece of paper. The importance of a contract lies in the verbal engagement. A paper may be burnt or torn, but a promise or a handshake cannot. A contract in the Chinese mind is, after one has felt the partner's pulse and evaluated the confidence he or she can invest, an engagement to do something together. Once the decision is made to do it, there is no turning back. Difficulties, unexpected details, problems of various levels and importance may happen, and they will be taken into consideration when the moment comes – probably face to face during a good meal, a glass (or more) of *bai jiu* (white alcohol) when ideas are clarified. A solution will undoubtedly be found because the partners have given their word. Some foreigners think that they can quit their position in China at any time, since they have not signed any paper. This is a serious mistake.

If they have accepted the job, they have accepted the contract.

In the last two or three years, contracts the way we foreigners understand them, often translated from foreign languages, have begun to circulate in different fields of activity in China. My publishers offer me contracts that are similar to those I sign in Canada, France, or Italy.

"A country governed by law" has become a reality in a few years. The government invests much effort in revising and improving the Chinese laws not only for the nation, but to adjust them to the general principles of the WTO member countries. The Law on Marriage of the People's Republic of China has been revised and finally voted on in 2001. It was amended, then submitted to the citizens who participated through various channels, examined again under the light of new propositions and following comments and remarks from citizens, and finally voted, sanctioned, and implemented. In a dynamic society, laws easily become obsolete and can no longer respond to the new situations of modern life, such as an important article of the revised Law on Marriage, which concerns family violence.

But what would be the use of laws if people did not know about their existence? The State has tried by all means to promote legal education among the people, to let the citizens know their rights and duties, to give them the means to respect the laws. Obviously, not all citizens have the necessary resources to do so, and the appropriate assistance has been instituted. The system, far from perfect and in constant evolution, has already served thousands of persons.

The State also organises the training of honest judges and competent lawyers, because there is a large loophole in this matter. Canada, for one, has subsidised a training project with excellent results. Laws finally exist where only indications and measures existed before, or even less, tradition. However, of two impartial judges one may inflict a 10-year prison sentence, the other, capital punishment. There is no jurisprudence. Verdicts vary from a region to another, from one court to another.

Opening a special issue on China of *Le Point* (France, December 21-28, 2001), I read, "If statistics are kept secret, we know that China holds the world record of capital executions." If that were so! Meanwhile, China has acknowledged a great number of charges for which capital punishment is inflicted, and it plans to reduce these in the next few years, but Roma was not built in one day...

Personally, I don't completely agree with a sentence that depends of "the amount" of stolen money, extorted, or involved in fraud. It's still *Le Point* that denounces: "Less than 50 grams of heroin, 15 years of prison. More than 150 grams, capital punishment." I understand that 50 grams often means that those using the heroin are using it personally, while 150 grams usually indicates that the owner is selling the drugs to other people and spreading an illegal substance: thus, a higher sentence. Even though, I find this shocking, certainly. On the other hand, rules exist, and criminals who try to defy them know the risks very well. All will not be caught, but those who are create a case law and an example. What a pity that some offenders escape the law because they hold power, a certain power: the power to improve oneself destiny or destroy oneself life.

The Lucky Number

In the 1990s, the Chinese word *gupiao* (shares) became very popular. Chinese people were discovering the stock exchange, and they bought as many shares as possible. The stock exchange is a recent institution in China, still badly managed and badly ruled. Investors often lost their money for that reason, not because of the market itself. *Gupiao* were once the object of comic dialogues, films, plays, and TV series.

Then came the lottery, which attracted many more players as it requires less investment. The new concept, after a period of hesitation about its moral aspect, became very popular. To the buyer of a single 2 yuan ticket, or for the one who spends hundreds of yuan, isn't the jackpot of 5 million yuan tempting? Almost half of the urban residents have bought tickets – 6% of the people in the whole country. From the 15 billion yuan revenue it produced in 2000, 85 to 100 billion are expected in 2010.

The first Beijing Sport Lottery, initiated in May 2000, yields an average of 20 million yuan at each new issuing. Following such a success, another kind of lottery was established benefiting welfare institutions. In Shanghai, in 1999, such a lottery produced 40 million yuan in sales. Then, the welfare lottery was implemented in Beijing, in May 2000.

Not only does this new industry yield direct profits, it provides jobs: 40,000, at least, 80% of which are for workers laid off by the State-owned enterprise reform.

The "New-New" Youth

The 2000-2001 "Report on Beijing Youth," based on a four-month enquiry of 16- to 35-year-old Beijingers, showed that these people try to find a balance between traditional culture and modern ideas, and have a more open and varied life than the previous generation. Among them, 17.8% are interested in politics, particularly in the battle against corruption, the promotion of honest politics, the protection of environment, Beijing's bid for the 2008 Olympic Games, the reform or social welfare system, and the problems related to public security.

Concerning religion, 68.9% declared that they believe only in science, while 21.6% have faith only in themselves. Their idea of family (60.7% of the young clearly choose marriage with one child, while 10% reject it) is an attempt at a rational, realistic concept. Over 80% think that one must respect the partner's secrets even after marriage, and about 75% agree with notarising (setting a legal contract) property before marriage.

Faithful to themselves, the contemporary young people live a free life and see themselves as the initiators of a new wave. Compared with traditional ideas, they show remarkable qualities: independence, liveliness, creativity, frankness, and searching for their truth.

The time has passed when exams served only to measure competence. In front of the practical experience required by employers, students find bookish knowledge less useful to the point that, sometimes, they forget that university knowledge will allow them to develop strongly in the long term. As in the current area of "knowledge economy," knowledge is renewed every five years, many of them prefer to participate in the social reality instead of losing time in books far from reality and that become outdated quickly.

Among recent graduates, 2% choose to say "no" to a job that seems too ordinary, which discourages their parents and teachers. Their choice is idealistic, and sometimes they place too much importance on their rights and not enough on their duties regarding society, as extolled in the traditional culture.

Do they deserve our confidence? The future will tell.

The Internet Presence

We have mentioned the spectacular evolution of the Internet in China, but I would like to discuss its influence on society. Students, even primary school children, *shang wang* (go on-line) to find information about topics they study, for part-time jobs, or a permanent job after graduation. Adults of all ages search for romance on the Web. Often, they establish a connection and a few months later, the people, often a great distance from each other, arrange to meet; it's not uncommon for a wedding to follow. A non-scientific survey showed that 50% of the couples who married at Spring Festival in 2002 had met on the Internet.

The Internet also serves commerce: all kinds of products and services are offered on and purchased on-line, but China lags behind the international level in this field. In one practical aspect, there is real progress: the possibility to reserve train and air tickets without having to leave the house. All this was unimaginable a few years ago.

Foreign Celebrations

During the final decade of the last century, the State repeatedly prohibited the celebration of foreign festivals, but who cared? Even though Chinese media continue not to publicise these festivals, I didn't hear any interdiction in the past three or four years. After the introduction of Mother's Day and Valentine's Day (in China, "Lovers' Day"), April Fool's Day and Hallowe'en have had lukewarm reception.

However, Easter has no hold on China; but who could resist the charms of Christmas? A social and commercial event even in traditionally Christian countries, Christmas in China is an opportunity for a sumptuous dinner in a great restaurant, with an orchestra, and to dance, sing, go out, drink, and have fun with friends. The Chinese have a deep sense of festivity, and Christmas gives them an opportunity to please themselves.

Since Chinese people have one more day off for each important festival, foreigners have two (previously, just one) for Christmas. They have the right to take them if their absence doesn't impede the normal workflow.

Year after year, Christmas gains in "perfection." The Western traditional decorations have appeared in stores, followed by artificial pine trees, and finally real trees, cut or potted, in 2001. In hotels, big building halls, an immense decorated pine tree glitters. Santa Klaus (*Shengdan Lao Ren* or Christmas Old Man) opens taxi doors. Midnight suppers are organised in hotels, and more and more Chinese attend them. Christmas is also seasoned the Chinese way: from September, markets offer foreign tourists Christmas ornaments to decorate the tree (1999), then cloisonnÈ bells (2000), and, finally, in 2001, huge angels, stars, and even crosses – a horrible hodgepodge of all the Christian symbols. Christmas has become a good commercial opportunity in China as well as anywhere else.

Nevertheless, when all the Christmas elements are reunited, there is still one missing: the Christmas spirit.

Stress

The major difference I found in life and work when I arrived in China in 1991 was the absence of pressure. Having endured it for long years when I was teaching, it was good to forget the race for efficiency and profitability, multiple meetings, and reports to establish and present; all these added to responsibilities inherent in my position.

Day after day, I have observed this developing in China, especially with the introduction of foreign enterprises, obliging the Chinese, once used to a different system, to accept and follow their pace of production. A French enterprise, for instance, had hired me to give French classes in the evening, twice a week for three months. The chosen students were requested to take the course, but their jobs at work remained unchanged. So, for each lesson, one-third of the registered students were absent on business trips, and those who were present had had no time to open their books from the last lesson. As for practising French in their daily work, it was only a dream, as their French directors themselves addressed the Chinese employees in English "in order to save time."

I look with sadness at these unaware Chinese who struggle with this new phenomenon: stress. In today's China, the workloads, ferocious competition, risks, and worry over employment have their effects on physical and mental health. People who have only time for survival are no longer an exception, unfortunately. Those who used to enjoy a relaxed life are now expected to do more in less time. Some lose control of their own lives, and, without thinking, gradually develop unhealthy habits, such as gulping down their meals (if those instant dishes or frozen food heated in a microwave can legitimately be called meals), and skipping the usual nap.

Appliances and services such as photocopiers, e-mail, and cellular telephones have clearly made work easier; but have made people slaves to time, and, as a result, they look for shortcuts everywhere. People become impatient if the elevator takes more than 15 seconds to arrive, and they repeatedly press the button, as though the number of presses will bring the elevator more quickly.

Even though a washing machine allows one to do other things simultaneously, and even though the airplane and car have replaced the train and bicycle, people still want to do more in the same amount of time; thus, their bodies face a challenge. One result may be cardiovascular disease. This is the ransom of modern society and people may avoid paying it, even after suffering total exhaustion, which alone may or may not bring a little wisdom. Until one has a negative experience from this extreme pressure, one doesn't easily agree to save one day a week for total rest – one evening out of seven for perfect relaxation alone, in company of one's spouse, or family. Moreover, a good mood and positive outlook are necessary for maintaining mental health, because they're conducive to the production of endorphins, which may alleviate mental and vascular pressure.

Considerable Improvements

A Canadian who had been in China for five months told me how rude she found the store clerks and how impolite the service was. So I enlightened her on the situation as it was 10 years before, realising myself how much progress had been accomplished.

The quality of products, particularly clothes and electrical appliances, was not quite up to standard. Still, all is not perfect, but there are fewer soles that detach from the shoe after a few minutes' walk, fewer socks of different lengths in the same pair, fewer buttons that remain in the hand at the first unbuttoning, fewer sweater necks through which the head cannot pass, and fewer ill-fitting sleeves the first time one puts on a shirt, not to mention more colour-fast clothing. Faulty appliances have caused several accidents in the country. When they sold the appliances, the stores didn't replace or repair them, or even refund the money. They couldn't explain to the customer how to contact the manufacturer, because "after-sales service" was absolutely unknown. If Haier Company (to name only one) has succeeded on the Chinese market, it is because it knew how to develop after-sales service and reach the level of its main international competitors.

Newly arrived foreigners in China don't see the difference between a large Chinese shopping centre or a supermarket and their counterparts in the world. They are unaware that the variety of products, their display, and their stock are something new in China's commerce.

Public transportation has also improved in every sense: number of bus lines, frequency, reserved lanes for buses, cleanliness, maintenance, and comfort (even heated or air-conditioned according to the season) of the vehicles – all for a ridiculously low rise in price, compared to the rise in service.

Concerning trains, besides comfort and quality, their speed increased on several lines, and China is the third country, after Germany and Japan, to build the magnetic suspension train. With being able to reserve a ticket a few days in advance and to do it at one of the many sales counters that are networked by computer, without having to queue for hours at the train station (ending with the answer "*meiyoule*" (sold out)), travelling has become more pleasant, even during the Spring Festival period, though it comes with many other difficulties.

The housing conditions of the Chinese people improve constantly. Comfortable and larger apartments are being built, equipped with central electric or natural gas heating, without the previous water or electricity shortage one day a week, alternating by district, and where telephone infrastructures already exist. Several work units can be had at a very low price, or with a loan that may be redeemed by a deduction of wages; banks also offer mortgages.

However, the Chinese people are not yet familiar with the concept of property; they still don't know how to take care of the common areas (what belongs to everyone doesn't seem to belong to anyone), such as the staircases, the yard, the incinerator, the foyer, so they deteriorate very quickly, while the inside of individual apartments is well-maintained by each family.

More and more apartments are accessible to foreigners to buy or rent, from the more luxurious and spacious, with house-keeping services and broadband Internet, to the more modest, but even the latter are much too expensive for the average foreigners who live here on local wages. The costs of these units in absolute numbers are equal to or higher than the price of an apartment in Manhattan, Toronto, or Paris.

Hygiene

Since 1991, I have observed major achievements in the area of hygiene: meat, milk, and eggs are often refrigerated. The staffs of restaurants, clinics, and hospitals wear gloves, and their clothes are cleaner than they used to be. Public restrooms also are more inviting and can now be found along the streets, in parks, stores, restaurants, and museums. Cleanliness has imposed itself in restaurants (tables, tableware, glasses, floors, and waiters' uniforms). Food sold in the streets and in other public places is covered or wrapped up.

Some of my family members who come to visit me every

two or three years are impressed, from one time to the next, by these changes.

But...

At the beginning of 2002, Chinese consumers were concerned mostly by the 10 following areas during 2001. According to the China General Administration of Industry and Commerce, these results come from the statistics analysed in matters of consumers' rights and interests protection, from the trials that occurred, and from data from information centres and 20 large cities in the country.

Their concerns were about counterfeit food products, bad telecommunication services, low quality of mobile telephone and services, lack of efficiency of public services, disputes concerning housing, defective manufacture of cars, cosmetics, false information, third-party swindles, and farmers' being overtaxed.

Around the Country

"Les voyages forment la jeunesse" (Travelling Educates the Youth)

I often tell my Chinese friends that they are lucky, because even without leaving their country, they may cross several climatic zones, from the tropical Hainan to the cold Harbin. They can enjoy the sunny beach near the sea as well as the snow and ice festival, take part in the international kite festival in Weifang or in the dragon-boat race in Guangdong, climb the Himalayas in Tibet, travel through the desert in Inner Mongolia, visit Guangxi's caves, Kunming's Stone Forest, Hangzhou's West Lake, Datong's Hanging Temple, the Ming Dynasty Yixian village in Anhui Province, and Banpo Village in Xi'an, which is no younger than 7,000 years old. They can view the splendid Dunhuang Buddhist grottoes in Gansu Province, the sacred Taoist and Buddhist mounts, the exceptional sugar loaf landscapes of Guilin, Huangshan Mountain's misty peaks, the frosted trees of Jilin, the water city of Zhouzhuang, Huangguoshu Falls in Guizhou Province, and recall the history of the Chinese nation born on the banks of the Yellow River – sometimes tormented, sometimes almost dry – and developed on the loess. They can be surprised by the modernity of Shanghai or the marvels of Shenzhen, a city born from nothing; they can find themselves almost in a foreign country among the Xinjiang's Uygur people or the Dai people in Xishuangbanna, or in paradise in the romantic Gulangyu Island, and discover several other wonders in the 34 provinces, autonomous regions, municipalities directly under the central government, and special administrative regions, and those of the 56 ethnic groups that inhabit China, this immense country, third in size in the world after Canada and Russia. Truly, I believe there is no other country on the globe that offers so much to discover, in terms of natural and human landscapes, of festivals and all kinds of activities, at any time of year.

China possesses the whole range of geographic landscapes; each region contains a cultural microcosm, and each ethnic group has its customs, its culinary art, its music, and its costumes. Everywhere I travelled in the country, I've tasted fruits and vegetables previously unknown to me (not to mention the ways in which they were prepared); I have seen new flora and fauna and different wildlife. Here, one sees peacocks and elephants and, there, wild donkeys, foxes, and tigers.

Remember that Beijing is not the whole China, and even after 10 or 20 years spent in a large city of the country, people cannot claim to know China.

Many lives and trips would be necessary to see everything. One could plan an art excursion (for example, ancient musical instruments, painting and sculpture, acrobats, Peking Opera and local operas), a handicraft outing (new year printings, paper cuts, four types of Suzhou embroidery, cloisonné), a gastronomic trip (Luoyang 24 soups banquet, imperial banquet, Beijing roast duck, beggar chicken, the "four cuisines" – Shandong, Sichuan, Guangdong, and Jiangsu), and yet another one for the ethnic habitats (Tujia's round houses in Fujian, Mongolian yurts), Yao nationality houses on pillars. Other excursions could include a cultural theme, such as martial arts, traditional medicine, tea, as well as apparel (those of the Manchus, the Tibetans, the Miao). There could be excursions for songs and dances (Uygur, Naxi), festivals (Nadam with the Mongols, Xoidun with the Tibetans, Water Splashing Festival with the Dai), religious rites (Taoist and Buddhist temples, pagodas, steles), and for natural landscapes, one ecological, one historical, and so on.

To date, I've set my foot in all the corners of the country except Qinghai and Guizhou, but I'm just waiting for the moment. I have seen poverty-stricken regions as well as economically advanced ones. If I visited a few provinces several times, such as Inner Mongolia, Yunnan, Ningxia, and Shanxi, it's not because I prefer them, but because my work, family, or activities such as tree planting called me there. In fact, where is my preference? This question arises all the time, and I haven't found the answer. Everywhere, there is something unusual, and, being a curious person, I find interest in every discovery.

Among the trips that impressed me more was a Spring Festival spent with a countryside family in Zhejiang Province, where my towel was frozen hard in the morning (inside my room); my first sojourn to Yunnan, which I was ready to quit after 30 hours on the train, while there were 27 more to endure before arriving in Kunming, and 36 others to reach Xishuangbanna; my holiday in Xinjiang (72 hours by train), where the Uygur people thought I was a Kazakh and the

Kazakh, a Uygur. Writing this stirs my memory, and I am tempted to enumerate many others...

Travelling without Leaving

Even in Beijing, one may go somewhere every weekend for years and he or she will not yet have seen all the possible sites. Besides the Great Wall and the Forbidden City, there are many parks, museums (about 90), temples, palaces, lakes and canals, residences of princes, historic or literary figures, attractions such as the Ethnic Minorities Park, the World Park (reproduction of the main world monuments), the Millennium Altar (*Shiji tan*), a wonder itself, where marvellous exhibitions are hold, the Fragrant Hills (*Xiang shan*) in the western section of the city, and so on.

Visiting historic, cultural, or natural sites, with a guide or reading by ourselves before and after the visit, how much one can learn! A single example: number 9, formerly reserved for the emperor, is a symbol of longevity because it is a homophone of "old" in Chinese, and also because it is the highest of simple numbers. This is why it has always been said that the Imperial Palace (Forbidden City) had 9,999 rooms, until 1994, when a detailed count revealed that there were actually 8,600. But, legend prevails, and no guide will dare tell you otherwise.

What one should not forget when visiting Beijing is the famous *hutong* or lanes, with their charming *siheyuan* (square-yard-houses.) I wish I could live in one of these, even though my mother can't believe it, which proves how even persons in the same family differ.

For relaxation I like nothing more than walking alone in a park of the capital or visiting a temple with its gardens and outbuildings. From the outside, we can't even imagine these oases of calm and beauty, hidden behind high walls, and this is correct: the peace found there must be earned, by entering these places humbly, step by step, in silence and meditation. Then, one can leave wistfully, revived but wishing the whole night could be spent there.

Travelling in Yunnan

In September 1993, since I had a 3-day weekend for National Day, I decided to spend it in Inner Mongolia, but I had an alternative plan before going to the train station in case no tickets were left. In fact, they were sold out. Same for Datong. Of the remaining on the list, I chose Qingdao, so I could enjoy the last days of sea bathing before the cold season. The train was to leave at 0:58 (the next day), and I forgot to change the date on my order form, which meant that I showed up to leave with a ticket dated the day before. Not only did I stay in Beijing, I lost the cost of the ticket (69 yuan at that time).

In the summer of 1992, I visited Yunnan Province. I was supposed to leave with four Chinese friends who changed their minds at the last moment for personal reasons: too much work, no time for holidays! Gathering all my courage, I decided that I would travel alone, then, for 57 hours.

The compartment was full of young athletes who'd been to Beijing for competitions. As soon as the train moved, they all installed their cups with toothbrushes and toothpaste on the window sill, their towels on the baggage shelves, and, on the table, their instant noodles and their tea jars. They opened bags containing boiled eggs, fruit, and cookies. After eight hours, I wondered whether I could tolerate the remaining 49 hours. During the night, the plains turned into mountains, corn fields became rice paddles. Sixteen stops in 3,000 km.

Early in the morning, the fast-food vendor began to circulate. I wanted a real Chinese breakfast: noodle soup, preserved vegetables, eggs, beans, tomatoes with sugar, cakes, grape, and soy milk.

There was no air conditioning in the compartment. Ice cream sold very well at the station where we stopped at 10:00, close to Wuhan. Temperature: 40 degrees Celsius.

After 30 hours, I reached my threshold of endurance. I was tempted to turn around, but I realized that I would have to spend the same time in another train without having seen anything of Yunnan. After all, the situation wasn't so bad: children don't mind foreigners, and I didn't have to undergo the avalanche of questions with which curious adults usually assail me, even kindly. They don't realise that if I talk with them for 10 minutes each, it's 12 hours a day that I'm answering, smilingly and in my bad Chinese, to their questions, which are always the same. Only the accents change. I finally understood the American who told me once, "When I travel, I don't know a single word of Chinese!"

I occupied the upper sleeper, third level, less than one metre from the ceiling. Wasn't that a triple advantage? My baggage, being on my bed, didn't need to be watched; moreover, no one sat on my bed during the day and I could lie down any time I wanted without being disturbed. Finally, the fan was very close to me (but too close to my throat, which I protected from its breeze).

In the afternoon on the second day, no water was available. Usually, people fill up their thermos from the furnace, at the end of the compartments. Sinks serve to wash clothes as well as the face, feet, and hair. Some people say that the lack of water is deliberate, in order to allow the vendors in the stations to sell more bottled water and soft drinks, and share the profits. If so, what about the non-potable water that's missing in the washrooms?

In the rough Guizhou Province's mountains, the train choked, slowed down, and stopped completely. What had happened? A farmer in his 30s had thrown himself on the tracks. The trip seemed to go by like an eternity. No matter! An old teacher told me that, in 1957, it would have taken 10 days to cover the same distance.

On board, people had the bad habit of throwing all the garbage through the windows. They had fun breaking bottles and jars on the stones along the railway. Styrofoam containers dotted the fields. A farmer erected a "sculpture" with all the non-biodegradable material carried by the wind to his field. The train staff kept cleaning and sweeping, but they also threw outside what should have gone into the dustbin. They themselves told the passengers to get rid of the waste through the window, even though it was written, "Please do not throw anything outside." Back in Beijing, I wrote a letter to the newspaper *China Daily* on this topic and suggested three ways to improve the situation, protect the environment, and offer a better image to the tourists. A few months later, a national campaign was launched. One year later, travelling by train, I saw changes; in fact, I reached Kunming in two and a half days in the late afternoon. After a short night at the hotel, because the next morning began at 5:00, I went on another odyssey: 36 hours toward Xishuangbanna in a bad and crowded bus. Three of us shared a seat for two, which was also broken and leaning to the right. The aisle was so packed with luggage that when the bus stopped for a few minutes, we couldn't stand up or go to the wash room, except in a case of extreme emergency and to the curses of all the other passengers. I was the only foreigner. It was only when we stopped at a hostel that night that some discovered that I spoke Chinese; from that moment, I had no rest until we arrived.

Returning to Kunming six days later – it took 48 hours to obtain a flight ticket to arrive in Beijing the same day that classes began. I had no regrets. That part of China, in the southwest, where 24 ethnic groups live, is one of the most interesting. The travelling problems were quickly forgotten after seeing so many wonderful sights.

A Few Days in Ningbo

I have visited Zhejiang Province four times, in every season, in 1985, 1993, 1999, and 2001. What a difference each time! The last time was in Ningbo, which is, since the highway has been opened, only one hour and a half from the provincial capital, Hangzhou.

Under the Tang Dinasty, Ningbo was called Mingzhou. In 1381, under the Ming Dinasty, the city received its current name, which means "calm wave." Ningbo was involved in commerce centuries ago. During the Tang Dynasty, it was a commercial port. In the 1980s, with the implementation of China's reform and opening-up policy, Ningbo resumed its vitality and in 1984, Ningbo was listed as one of 14 opened coastal cities and in 1987 was approved by the State Council to have economic administrative rights at the provincial level. The "Ningbo Clique" refers to Ningbo businessmen who live here or have returned from overseas. The Clique developed between 1573 and 1621, the most prosperous period in Chinese commercial history. About 300,000 Ningbo Chinese are scattered throughout 64 countries and regions in the world; 800 are celebrities in all fields. Ningbo people are proud of their Clique because the members have accumulated extensive intellectual and financial resources. After enjoying success overseas, these entrepreneurs made substantial donations to their region to stimulate the economy and develop education, and they have returned to help personally. According to the municipal government, 400 members of the overseas Clique have invested 600 million yuan in 2,000 projects. The Clique built Ningbo University, and 300 primary and middle schools, about 100 hospitals, kindergartens, seniors' homes, children's centres, libraries, research institutes, and transportation facilities. The Clique has invested US$290 million in nearly 200 enterprises in Ningbo.

The Tianyi Pavilion, built 400 years ago, is one of the top four or five ancient libraries in China. Its well-ventilated wooden tower, which is fire and moisture resistant, made it possible for its 300,000 volumes to be preserved. It was built by Fan Qin who had travelled to many places and acquired all kinds of books. At 80, he divided his property in two parts: 10,000 taels of silver, and books. His elder son chose the tower and books as his heritage, being aware of the extent of his involvement; his descendants would have to watch over the collection and their potential reneging could have brought shame to the family. So, he strictly forbade anyone to enter the pavilion under threat of severe punishment.

Presently, Ningbo has four institutes of higher education: the Foreign Language Institute with its imposing architecture, one vocational school and two adult learning schools – altogether about 20 universities, colleges, and specialised schools.

I often thought that, in China, I could live only in Beijing but I recently discovered another city where I would not refuse to work. Ningbo, in the east of Zhejiang Province, has a population of 5.33 million inhabitants on 9,365 square km.

Its urban region of 1,033 square km hosts 20% of its population, a balanced distribution. Because the city is quite small, it's possible to travel from the centre to the suburbs in a few minutes. Public transit is efficient and taxi fares are low. The annual per capita disposable income of urban dwellers averages 9,492 yuan and for rural residents, 4,798 yuan.

The province has adopted the slogan: "Clear water, blue sky, green earth." This programme extends to the whole province but has been realized already in Ningbo City. During one stay there, I noticed a mild, pleasant breeze that didn't raise any dust... No need to shine my shoes every day in Ningbo! The city is very green with wide, plush lawns and artistically tended shrubs, well-maintained trees in ever-increasing numbers, and steel and cement sculptures; all contribute to a peaceful and beautiful environment. Moreover, real estate is flourishing in Ningbo. Housing is superior to many cities in the country and apartments are spacious, well-designed, and clean, and their prices are affordable.

On my way to Fenghua, on the seashore of the East China Sea, on an air-conditioned bus with a safety belt for each seat, I was delighted by the marvellous scenery: gorgeous fields of various plants and typically southern species of vegetables, hills, rivers, and streams. I soon arrived at Xikou where I visited the residence where Chiang Kai-shek lived with his adoptive uncle. The place was very pleasant; one could rest in fresh air perfumed with the scent of magnolias and jasmine and appreciate the surrounding landscape. Fortunately the wonderful fragrance didn't prevent me from contemplating the beauty of the mountains and trees.

The other residence where Chiang Kai-shek used to spend his holidays with his family is even more beautiful. Both are

located in the heart of panoramic sites. I especially appreciated the visit to Hemudu Neolithic village site, one of the
cradles of Chinese civilisation about 7,000 years old, just as
the Banpo site in Xi'an, which reveals a different civilisation.
Because of climatic reasons, the Banpo houses are round, with
a structure of wooden posts set deep in the ground. Their walls
are of dried mud, while those of Hemudu's elevated houses,
with a subtropical climate and elephants and crocodiles, are
made of straw and wicker plaits. These houses are very large;
the whole clan could live and work there. No clothes or ornaments were found on the Hemudu site and there are no clues
about funerary rites, either, but it was a matriarchal society,
with the sun and two birds as a totem. These figures are reproduced on decorative objects as well as on wooden knives
and porches.

The village was discovered accidentally in 1983 by peasants who were cultivating the fields. Two excavations, in 1973
and 1977, on 2,800 square m of the total 40,000, brought to
the light 6,700 objects: tools of production in bone, stone, or
wood; cooking utensils; human and animal skeletons; cultivated rice and wild fruit; and even a small clay sculpture of a
pig. Clearly, this is one of the most important archaeological
discoveries in the world. For China, Hemudu summarises the
civilisation of the Yangtze while Banpo is the substance of
the Yellow River banks' civilisation.

Visiting Shanxi

Shanxi is another province that I've visited several times
– twice to plant trees with 200 volunteers from Beijing on the
banks of the Yellow River and in the bare mountains.

We were welcomed like heroes, complete with a local

band. In reality, our efforts were meagre compared with those of the local workers who had dug the holes in advance; we only had to cover the roots of young trees. But any fatigue, aches, and pains are quickly forgotten in such a splendid landscape: the Hukou Falls, which can be seen on the backs of 50-yuan bills. I can still hear the falls roar and feel on my skin the mist of the cascades, laden with yellow sand.

Another time, I went to rest a few days in Pingyao. A long weekend is enough. Overnight from Beijing, one arrives the next morning to the little city in the heart of the province. It is easy to find accommodations at a reasonable price. Visitors can taste, inexpensively, "*Pingyao niu rou*" (beef) and all kinds of dishes with amazing names such as "*kao laolao*", which awaken the imagination and fills the stomach.

Pingyao's origin traces back to the Ming Dynasty and is well-preserved. It has been designated by UNESCO as a treasure of the world. It is a pleasure to stroll about its streets and chat with the locals who sit outside their doors and work on crafts, such as paper cuts or embroidery. If one stops to examine the architecture, they will kindly invite you to visit their large homes, with their vast courtyards full of trees and flowers and where red peppers on a thread hang to dry.

The Guo family are educated people who possess great knowledge in Chinese medicine, painting, calligraphy, poetry, philosophy, etc. have made *huang jiu* (grain alcohol) for eight generations.

Pingyao, an ancient city of the wealthy, was where the first Chinese shares (*gupiao*) were issued – as early as 1821. The place has retained its past noble heritage. About 10 km from there, one can easily reach Qixian by bicycle. This is where Zhang Yimou filmed *Wives and Concubines*. Guides explain the history of this incredibly huge property that was once the residence of a single family.

Then, one can go to Taiyuan by bus or minibus, and reach Wutai Mountain, one of the five Buddhist mountains of China. Along the roads, the trees, golden or green according to the season and the fields of young shoots or of yellow straw against a backdrop of mountains paint a superb portrait.

The first time I went to Shanxi, I was not expecting so much beauty! I must say that Shanxi Province is one of the wonders of this country. My most recent visit to Shanxi was in 2001; we were hosts of the provincial government. After completion (National Day 2002), the 299-km Beijing-Datong highway will permit a round trip in only one day.

Just as several other large Chinese cities, Datong made remarkable progress in recent years. I can see this by comparing my recent photos with those taken six years ago.

The Yungang caves are a tribute to heaven and humankind. Parts of the caves are under renovation because stone fragments have fallen recently. Imagine that more than 1,500 years ago only a rocky mountain stood hereÖ nothing else. Inspired by his faith, Buddhist monk Tan Yao inaugurated the sculpture of the rock as a token of respect and, during the following dynasties, the work continued until there were 53 caves with 51,000 sculptures or high-relief figures of Buddhas, bodhisattvas, pusas and other religious characters, and 23,000 bas-reliefs. Thousands of craftspeople worked there, leaving to posterity Buddhas of all sizes – from the smallest, measuring just 2 cm, to the tallest, 17 m, which is in No. 5 cave. Criteria of health and beauty have changed throughout history, so one can see many fat Buddhas, made under the prosperous era of the Tangs, and others, skinny and gracious, sculpted in leaner periods.

The Yungang caves rank third in the world after those in

India and Afghanistan, the latter of which were destroyed by the Taliban. The Dunhuang grottoes are mostly known for their painted frescoes.

The sky that day was almost as blue as in Tibet, contrasting sharply with the pollution of the city. In the fresh air and sunshine, it was good to meditate on human creativity, which 1,600 years ago, without modern tools or high technology, introduced civilization into the world. The man-made caves are a temple dedicated to human intelligence and patience.

Datong's cultural resources are endless. What can I say, for example, about the Huayan Temple, built in 1038, one of the best-preserved constructions of the Liao Dynasty (916-1125); about the Xuankong Nine-dragon Screen, the greatest (45.5 m long by 8 m high and 2.02 m thick) and the most ancient of the three remaining screens of this kind in China (the other two are in Beijing, in Beihai Park and the Forbidden City); about the Hanging Temple, which was built on the side of a sheer vertical cliff; about the biggest wooden pagoda in China, the Yingxian pagoda built under the Liaos?

During this trip, we visited residential complexes, schools of all levels, several enterprises (drugs, ceramic, porcelain, fish, dairy products, textiles, etc.), an open coal mine, the Datong Economic and Technical Development Zone, and Shuozhou, a city born from almost nothing, etc. In a few days, we had an outline of the city and the inhabitants, including housing, work, education, and industry.

Ningxia, Small and Unknown

As Ningxia Hui Autonomous region is my husband's birthplace, we naturally go quite often. Not only foreigners but even Chinese people could not see Ningxia on the map a few years ago. Then, the government started to promote it, and now tourism is becoming its main industry but this is a recent trend.

Gourmands may take a gastronomic trip to Ningxia. Mutton meat (or goat) is much better in Yinchuan than in Beijing, and still superior in Guyuan, in the middle of the Autonomous Region. Some people refuse to taste mutton meat because of its smell, they say. I assure you that in Guyuan, it has no unpleasant smell. Moreover, in Guyuan, it is 40- to 50-day-old lamb that is served, and is prepared in different ways: roasted, in a sauce, stewed, sliced, with the bone, etc.

I have been surprised to find such large and rich museums in Ningxia, which is not yet very developed as a region. The Ningxia Museum, in the capital, holds precious relics of the Western Xia, which are protected by the State. Mostly original, these pieces are very well-preserved; they include ceramics, Buddhist statuettes, and *tanka* (Tibetan religious paintings). The smallest printed Coran in the world (3 cm) can be viewed in this museum, as well as an ox skull with its horns, dating back 30,000 years. Finally, the numerous engravings on the Helan Mount side can be seen here; they were crafted by nomads who bequeathed the shepherd scenes of their lives. The largest measures about 1 m by 1.5 m. These precious painted and engraved images prove that, at least 6,000 years ago, human beings – human civilisation – lived in Ningxia.

I was particularly interested in the history of Western Xia writing. The characters form a system even more complex than the Han. Analysis is still ongoing. Li Fanwen, chairman of the Ningxia Social Sciences Academy, leads the study in this matter. Born in Shaanxi in 1939, he has devoted more than 40 years to studying Xia's language, and his

Xia-Chinese dictionary, compiled over the course of 27 years and based on homophones, is the key that opened the door to the mystery.

Visiting mosques, which number as many as the churches in Roma, is fascinating. The Nan Guan great mosque of Yinchuan was the starting point of our pilgrimage to "Mecca." This temple was built with the local Muslim community's offerings. I was very moved, on my first visit in 1996, to see the names of all donators engraved on steles, not only those who had offered substantial amounts but those who could offer only 0.3 yuan.

The Muslim's life is centred around the mosque, and in Ningxia, we had an opportunity to get to know them better, to meet several members of their community, to taste their hospitality as well as their snacks and the "eight treasures" tea they prepare sometimes with honey or rose jam instead of sugar.

Ningxia culture is strongly influenced by the Western Xia Dynasty. Who are these kings? They descended from the Dang Xiang ethnic group, which is now extinct. They reigned in the west of the country when the Songs dominated the east. Their realm included today's Ningxia, a large part of Gansu, north of Shaanxi, west of Inner Mongolia, northeast of Qinghai, and east of Xinjiang. Their dynasty includes 10 emperors, between 1038 and 1222, the year they were overthrown, after five unsuccessful attempts, by the Mongols and the Yuan Dynasty.

The 270 picturesque and astonishing tombs of the Western Xia cover endless land. They look like conical anthills. In fact, these cones are not the tombs themselves but the covered ruins of Buddhist pagodas with glazed tile roofs, which were ransacked and burnt by the Mongols, while the tombs remain underground.

The Xia had particular mythical figures, reproduced on what appear to be columnar bases; they are animal-like, with bulging eyes and heavy, pendulous breasts. What they represent remains a mystery.

Ningxia is also a place for fun, and the best destination for that is Sha Hu (Sand Lake), in the heart of the desert, 56 km northwest of the capital Yinchuan. The lake is surrounded with sand hills where one can walk bare foot. There, several activities are open to tourists: camel riding, sledding on the sand and climbing back in a cable car, flying over the valley by pulley, parachuting, playing basketball, driving a dune buggy on the sand, etc.

I have mentioned only the areas around Yinchuan, but the whole region is interesting. Ningxia is surrounded by four deserts, but not only coal and sand grow in Ningxia Hui Autonomous Region, which is one of the five granaries of the country. Ningxia also exports its meat, poultry, and dairy products to the neighbouring provinces. This has not come all naturally; government, scientists, and brave and vigorous men have contributed to it. Presently, the region is in full exploitation in the wave of "the great development of the West."

Thanks to a good irrigation system and much sunshine, Ningxia has been able to develop its agriculture. Moreover, Ningxia has 9 of the 10 varieties of coal known in China, a range of 50 minerals, the exclusive black and green Helan Mountain stone, and precious medicinal herbs such as liquorice.

The miracle of the desert has occurred in Shapotou, at the extreme southeast of the Tengger Desert; works have been classified by the United Nations among the world 500 most important for environmental protection. Seeing these forests or these flourishing orchards, it's difficult to believe that only sand was there previously. Medicinal herbs are also cultivated in the deserts, and vineyards, using French and Italian methods, produce excellent wines that are not available outside the regions because they are not produced in great volume yet.

The Roof of the World

The magic and mysterious Tibet... I had dreamt of it for so long before getting my chance to go in 1994, with another foreigner working with me at CCTV, and a Chinese staff member. Even with the risk of "altitude sickness" I wanted to experience it. On the morning of August 4, when we landed in Lhasa Airport, the air was fresh, at 3600 m of altitude. At first, we felt as though we were wearing marshmallow shoes and bouncing like astronauts on the Moon. But soon after, we fell no more disturb, except a kind or cervix pressure without consequence. The important thing was to rest the first day and move slowly.

My husband, who had been in Tibet for long sojourns, has a different experience from mine. When one arrives by truck from Chengdu or by bus from Golmud, he or she gets used to altitude little by little. When the bus becomes engulfed in the mud, passengers must get out and push. A few seconds of effort are enough to make the heart beat quickly, as though it were going to burst.

On the other hand, we covered about 100 km by jeep, from the airport to the city, often stopping to take photos and admire nature. The surroundings seem desert-like, but as soon as we set down one foot, toothless old men and charming children who could only pronounce the word "bonbon" (candy) surrounded us. We had not thought to bring any, but we had apples and cookies for them. I was no longer the target as a foreigner, because Tibetans examined the Han Chinese as well.

I could finally see with my own eyes the deep azure, and small clouds of a brilliant white floated by. Every day, the sun shone until 16:00; then, with extraordinary punctuality, the sky became overcast in a second, and a thunderstorm erupted. At 18:00, everything became once again serene.

Tibetans have always astonished me by their ability to wear, in summer or winter, a coat of mutton skin held at the waist by a large, woollen belt and into which they put one sleeve for comfort while working. They don't seem to sweat in the summer or freeze in the winter. Monks also, in their wine-red tunics, always have one bare arm. Women wear long skirts, and, after marriage, a vividly coloured apron made of three sections with horizontal stripes.

On most days, they wear several kilos of jewellery: silver, copper, brass, or gold necklaces, decorated with coral, agate, turquoise, and other magnificent stones that are indigenous to Tibet. Their earlobes are stretched by the weight of their earrings, some with holes through which a drinking straw could pass.

Few foreigners know that the Tibetan population is composed of several sub-groups: Kangba, Anduo, Lhasa, etc. Other ethnic minorities also live in Tibet, especially the Muslim Hui and Sala, and the Han people. Kangba people, originally from Sichuan, are the men who most impressed me with their high stature and fierce bearing. Their long hair is intermingled with red or black woollen thread with pompons, which circle their heads.

Women are nice and round but not fat, and men, generally

well-proportioned. Their skin is burnished copper by the sun and the summit winds. They look at you directly, and their smile penetrates you. Extroverts by nature, Tibetans are boisterous; they like to laugh, sing, and play late into the night.

All the time I spent in Tibet, I felt as though I was in close contact with nature. Sitting on the grass writing my impressions, I looked at the 40-cm long goldfish practising their high jumps in the pond. A dragon-fly rested on my notebook. It was as though each plant looked at me and talked to me and that each stone was alive. Yaks were new to me, and dogs impressed me by their sheer numbers. What a wonderful place, so close to the sky, to concentrate and practise meditation!

Tibetans respect animal life of any kind, which is why there are few wild dogs in Lhasa. Every day, someone feeds them. If a fly is an annoyance in the house, they will guide it outside. If a fly falls into the water, legs up, they will save it. Even mice live harmoniously with these human beings.

A local tour guide confided in me how painful he found it was for him to show foreigners around Tibet because of their prejudices, which are so deeply rooted that they see reality through distorted lenses. I myself have felt such distortion when facing the questions people ask me in Canada or in Europe about Tibet. I notice that people don't listen to me; they just look for a word to confirm what they think they know. An example: in Lhasa, about 40 prisoners were taken to the public square where an official read their names before the crowd, identifying their charges, and stated their verdicts. (This is done regularly for open justice and to serve as a deterrent.) Then, the prisoners went back on the trucks to return to prison. Foreign tourists told my husband that "China was striking hard at the Tibetans preaching independence."

They had not understood a single word, but, based on their prejudices, they had filled in the situation. The prisoners were, in fact, charged for a variety of crimes – mostly theft, fraud, or unauthorised sale of merchandise. There were only two Tibetans among them; the others were almost all Han people, some from Sichuan for working, and Qinghai merchants of Hui nationality. Very few Westerners can distinguish one Asian person from another, and even fewer, a Tibetan from a Han.

I expected to see more Hans in Tibet. During the season migration period, they account for more than 10% of the population. Tibetans are not naturally inclined to business. In the neighbouring province of Sichuan, unemployment is high. Sichuan citizens have seized a ripe opportunity, and almost all restaurants belong to them. The farmers sell their products to Lhasa. Seasonal workers leave with the last of the tourists.

For the Tibetans who live in a "theocracy" Buddhism is a way of life. Tambourines, bells, drums, cymbals, 108-bead rosaries, little colourful flags printed with sutras, prayer wheels, barley seeds sounding on copper plates, typical sound horns are all objects that help the dialogue between humans and divinity. In Tibetan Buddhism, all beings have lives that deserve equal respect. I've noticed that it differs from Chinese, Japanese, Nepalese, and Vietnamese Buddhism. Religious practice is so deeply rooted in Tibetan lives, that prayers are continuous.

Tibetans go to temples, burning incense and adding butter in lamps with the knife hanging from their belt or a spoon. Everything is greasy and imbued with the smell of butter, especially the wooden or metallic rails without which steep, sudden stairs would be hard to navigate. They always circulate clockwise (1, 2, 3, 4, ...), also in Barkhor Street, the most animated place in Lhasa where all merchants have their stalls, even those from Xinjiang and from Nepal.

I have visited hundreds of temples around China, but what I call "the Tibetan experience" is something that cannot be articulated, the day of the "great *tanka* exhibition," an immense tapestry with an effigy of the Buddha. At 18:00, 40, 000 pilgrims, solemn and meditating, walked toward the mountain, throwing scented herbs on heaps of *mani* (flat stones making a stake). Once a favourable spot for observing was found, each one sat, silent. More than 100 monks transported on their shoulders the *tanka,* which goes out only once a year. Another hundred pairs of arms were needed to pull up the *tanka* with cables. At 20:30, all was finished. In the greatest calm, some went to touch with their forehead to the sacred image, others returned home, happy and peaceful. Never I had felt such a deep communion with humankind. Suddenly, I found myself in front of a woman around my age. We spontaneously took each other's hands, and I pronounced the only Tibetan expression I knew, "*Trashidele*" (greeting-blessing). We smiled and departed, each deeply moved.

It is good that, somewhere in the world, persons are happy because they have no desire. Therefore, they have no disappointments, no disillusions. Is it our duty or an imposition to give them what they don't ask for? This is a question that foreign "missionaries" (not officially sent by churches) should consider. Tibet is now fashionable. People are interested in this corner of the world, but don't understand what goes on. Are the statements of journalists who just pass through weighted in gold because they report the general current of prejudice?

My husband and I have several Tibetan friends, in Tibet and in Beijing, and Han friends who are tibetologists, sociologists, educated and open-mind people. A Han artist, from Shanxi, lives and works in Lhasa. A few years ago, he was granted six months in Germany with a fully equipped studio. Thirty days after he had arrived in Europe, he abandoned everything and came back to China; he missed Tibet.

Lhasa's urbanisation requires, as elsewhere, sacrificing something for progress. Here, protection; there, demolition; there is no other way. However, it is wonderful to see, from the Potala Hill, the residential quarters in the north, knowing that 30 years ago, only bog could be found there.

Compared with the Chinese style high-rise apartment buildings, Tibetans prefer the flat house for one family. Overall, only administrative services, enterprises, hotels and supermarkets are in big buildings. Tibetans build their own houses in 80% of the cases. What surprises me every time I enter a Tibetan house in Gansu, Sichuan, Yunnan, or Tibet is the space! Something that could raise envy in many Chinese, in cities especially.

Tibet's development is constant, fast, and impressive. A new industry, tourism, is very promising.

Spring Festival in the Countryside

I will never forget one trip. When I arrived in Hangzhou, a surprise was waiting for me: two former students instead of the expected one had come to welcome me. Since it was almost noon, they took me to a restaurant to have me sample local specialties such as "beggar chicken," which is a whole chicken wrapped in a lotus leaf and slowly baked, shrimp with tea leaves, 30-cm long eggplant as thin as a finger, lotus root stuffed with sticky rice, and a soup with *chuncai,* a vegetable which was new to me, very soft, milky and tender tofu that I never tasted anywhere else, and fish from West Lake.

Immediately after, I left for Xianju County, meaning "the Immortals' residence," with the student who was taking me to his family. It all would be fine, just an 8-hour bus ride. My guide, Ying Yuanma, my former student of French, told me many things about Zhejiang Province; for example, that Hangzhou was famous for silk, fans, tea, and scissors.

At 21:00, we arrived at his hometown, Jiang'ao. At this hour, from the station, there were only pedicabs. The trip was about 5 km, of which more than half was through the fields. There was no paved road. It had rained the day before, and there were many holes and lots of mud.

In Jiang'ao, at night, there was no artificial light but the stars; I had never seen so many stars in my life! They were not small specks in the dark but large luminous spots, bunched together, with little space between each. What a pleasure it was to brush my teeth under the stars – outside, of course, because there was no water inside.

About the toilet – I felt too shy to use the large terracotta bowl during the day with people around. Afterward, its contents were used to fertilize the fields, already green in February. I can't say I made an important contribution; when nature called me, I asked it to wait when I would be somewhere in town.

In Xianju, the tradition to welcome someone is by offering a sweet soup made with lychees and three poached eggs. I knew that it was not polite to refuse. Xiao Ying had not eaten anything at home to be able to help me eat my soup. At first, I was hungry, so I enjoyed this excellent and nutritious "snack." But after 24 eggs in four or five days, I could not stand to even look at a hen.

It was Spring Festival, and the six children of the family, with their spouses and children, had arrived at their parents' home. We ate three full course meals every day: pork, chicken, duck, fish, and snail. It's also a local Spring Festival tradition to eat many kinds of bread, evenly sliced and dried on a smouldering fire for 24 hours. This bread is a little sweet, like all the local food. When I left, Ying's good mother filled my luggage with it.

A baby was born in Ying's family. So, I learned how the Chinese chose a name, and other rites about birth. Every day I discovered cultural elements such as, in the kitchen, the woman's place is before the *zao* (kitchen range). The man stands behind the stove where he adds rice straw little by little. A man and a woman can't sit together behind the *zao* unless they are a couple. From time to time, water is poured in the stove through a little door, so there is always hot water available from a faucet in the front.

In the south of Yangtze, houses are not heated. I was given

the best room. Nevertheless, when I washed myself, the water in the basin became cold before I finished, and in the morning, I found my towel frozen hard in the room. Sleeping inside is worse than sleeping outside, with no paper even in the windows to act as a buffer for the cold and the doors did not close tightly. I usually awoke at 6:30, but I needed another hour to gather the courage to get out of bed. I could have heated my clothes under the blankets and dress before getting up, as I used to do in Italy, but, in fact, I slept fully dressed...

We visited a factory that produces more than 1,000 kinds of wooden arts and crafts. It's a family enterprise, whose kind members even invited us to share their dinner. All the relatives came to the factory that day because grandma and grandpa, who lived there, had prepared a huge meal (they said "an ordinary meal", but I counted 18 dishes) for more than 20 people.

In the evening, the women chatted and ate seeds, while men played cards and smoked. Sometimes I had to remind myself that I was in China, not Italy, because all I could see were similarities to ancient Italian customs.

I spent my last two days in Hangzhou and then flew to Beijing, where I found the air very dry. What a change! I took off my sweater and opened all the windows; as a result, I caught a cold.

As a foreigner, I've been greatly privileged to have stayed in the Zhejiang's countryside for one week, among authentic people, discovering the 807 million farmers of China. This page had been missing in the book of my life; now I think I understand China a little better.

Shaanbei, Another Planet?

My most recent discovery inside the Chinese frontier before the publication of this book is Shaanbei. For the Chinese people, February 11, 2002 was like December 31 for the Westerners. Firecrackers began to explode at 18:00 (in Beijing, in authorised places but also in illegal and dangerous places) and fireworks filled the air around 21:00. If I could hear, I could not see. I was in front of my computer, trying to finish a 5-page translation so that I could have free time during the one-week holiday. My husband also was working on the last cartoons of the last edition of the year since daily and weekly papers don't wait and don't enjoy "real" holidays. So, we entered the Year of the Horse without experiencing it much. The next day, as almost everyone had returned to his or her family hometown, it was easier to buy a train ticket, and we travelled in ideal conditions to Ningxia, my husband's native place, a 20-hour distance from Beijing, two hours less than last year – a noticeable progress.

A young couple accompanied us. Both had a driving licence. After the first day with family members, we borrowed a taxi whose owner had decided to take some days off, and left for Shaanbei, the northern part of Shaanxi Province (of which Xi'an is the capital). The distance between the two provinces can be marked obviously by the last toll booth, where the highway ends suddenly. Shaanbei is one of the poorest regions of China, all in arid mountains (800 m). The subsoil hides coal and oil, but the surface is covered with scrubs and thorns, and the desert devours it in big bites. Shaanxi is also included in the project "give the fields back to the forest": the State provides cereal to the farmers who, instead of cultivating infertile soil, plant trees and take care of them.

Spring Festival really lasts 15 days in the rural regions, ending with the Lantern Festival, contrary to cities. Being less busy during this period, farmers have time to rest and enjoy themselves. Stores, restaurants, and hotels were closed, as Shaanbei is not a tourist region. We, three Chinese and I, the foreigner, became the actors on whom all eyes turned, even the eyes of the *yangge* dancers (group dance with colourful costumes, and fans) and *yaogu* (belt drum) dancers, typical local performers.

For three days we only had Sichuan cuisine! Why? The owners of these restaurants who didn't succeed in getting a train ticket in the festive period to go back to their home-towns decided to stay to serve their few customers. Hotels, even the best ones in each city, opened two rooms for us when we were able to inspire pity in them, but they were rooms without heat or water (hot or cold). They gave us a thermos filled with boiling water, but without a basin, so it was a little difficult to wash ourselves. We could not even use the toilet as there was no water in it, and we had to go outside in the dark and cold night. The towels had not been changed, and the blankets were moist. We survived because we really wanted to be on this trip.

During our itinerary of more than 1,000 km, we viewed several sections of the Great Wall, built, in this province, of compressed earth layers. We even visited the largest watch-tower (four storeys) of the Wall, Zhenbei Tai. It was built during the Warrior States period and rebuilt in 1607 under the Ming Dynasty to protect the north from invaders, as its name indicates, The Huns (probable ancestors of today's Hungarians) have been living in the region for three hundred years under the Han Dynasty, often repelled and finally expelled in 91. At a certain distance, always at a height, another watchtower served in receiving Mongol delegates who came to discuss politics and military matters, as well as offer gifts to the emperor of China. For several kilometres, the Great Wall serves as a frontier between Ningxia and Inner Mongolia.

The first day, after a stop in Yanchi, we covered 300 more km, 80 of which were in a dense fog; the stars were too distant to light the road winding in the mountains.

The following day, from Yuhe we went to Yulin. From time to time, we got out of the car to see, for instance, an old abandoned temple but where incense had been burning not long before. Couplets traced in black or gold characters on red paper had been stuck on both sides of the doors by mysterious hands as there had been on each door of Shaanbei. Inside, frescoes, with still vivid and clear colours, had all lost their heads during the Cultural Revolution (1966-1976). We also visited Hongshi Xia (red stone gorge) with its Buddhist caves on one side of the river and famous figures' calligraphies on the opposite cliff.

Eighty kilometres later, we were in Jiaxian, where we saw two processions at the same time: one a funeral, the other a wedding, and so in the following days; we had never seen so many dead and so many new couples in such a short period. According to the local custom, when a person dies, the family installs a square linen tent along the sidewalk and places in it the photo of the dead, and friends and acquaintances come to pay homage and offer their condolences to the family.

The third day, we left at 7:30 for Ansai, a famous city of popular culture. We took many hours to covering the 260 km because it had snowed. We stopped in Mizhi, a small town, the birthplace of Li Zicheng, who had led his army of rebel peasants to Beijing in 1644, and other historical figures. Suide, on contrary, is known for its stone sculptures; pairs of lions of all styles and sizes lined the street.

In Zhejiaping, we took part in a village festivity and tasted local delicacies at the market. It was the *"chu wu,"* fifth day of the new year, and on this date, several popular activities take place. Not before 17:30 did we reach Ansai, a developed small town with an Internet Café, five or six storeys of modern houses, several stores, and billboards. Just days before, we had seen only *yaodong* (caves and cave dwellers), the typical Shaanbei architecture, which are houses dug in the yellow earth of the mountains, with doors and windows on the front only. They are very comfortable, warm in winter and cool in summer, and inside, they are like the other houses made of stone, wood, or brick. Often, the front is finished with brick or decorative tiles. Their doors and windows are detailed with sculpted wooden patterns, lines with translucent paper, on which paper cuts – a local craft – are applied.

Despite a few kilometres of unpaved road and some ditches, the roads are good. Three times we were stopped by a herd of goats that took all their time to stretch, at a call from their shepherd, and looked at us shamelessly, as though we were intruders.

The Ansai Museum director, whom we disturbed at home, was kind enough to open the museum for "the friends from afar," according to Chinese hospitality. There, we admired paper-cut works, embroidery on clothes and ornamental objects, calligraphies, naive or peasant paintings, toys and masks, as well as some prehistoric potteries found in the region. In Ansai, more than 100 persons have mastered the art of paper cutting, and classes are given once a year. Hou Xue Zhao is one of these; she also paints and makes little stuffed animals of cloth. At 48, she is a grandmother. Two of her five sons and their father were in Zibo, in the east of the country, where they had been invited to perform *yangge* and *yaogu*.

Finally, the last day there was a relentless sunshine when we reached Yan'an, where Mao Zedong established his headquarters in 1935 and settled down for a decade, heading the operations of the People's Army.

Unfortunately, the return was long and we had to arrive in Yinchuan before the evening. Never in my life had I seen so many mountains in so short a time. The greenery had not yet been awakened by spring; all was still greyish-yellow. Landscapes were impressive, and I felt as though was on an undiscovered planet.

At twilight we left the mountains, a little before entering Ningxia. At that moment, I remembered the pig Zhu Bajie's observations in *Pilgrimage to the West*: *Shan lian shan / Lu wan wan / Shenme shihou cai neng zou chu shan?* (Mountain after mountain / Curve after curve / when can we go out of the mountains?)

At home, my father and mother-in-law were waiting to boil the *jiaozi* (stuffed dumpling) that they had been preparing all day for us. And there was also my train ticket obtained at the last moment through an influential friend. I would leave for Beijing the next day, only half a day late. My three companions could wait for the traffic to ease and take a collective breath.

Opening New Eyes on China

The Meaning of the Word "Propaganda"

This word, in Western countries, provokes knowing smiles or weary scorn. It is necessarily associated with communist countries and is almost, if not frankly, a synonym of "lie." It frightens some, and people try not to hear it. I remember very well the idea I had of it myself before living in China. I was, as well as most of my peers and fellow citizens, unconscious of being a victim of the word, even though I lived far away from communism. The situation is even more dangerous when one does not suspect it. Many people of capitalist countries believe what their media and governments declare to be absolute truths, especially when they talk about what happens in other countries.

Tell them, for instance, that Chinese citizens enjoy religious freedom, that the State allows and respects normal religious activities and protects the legitimate rights and interests of the religious groups, that freedom of religion and equality in rights for all believers are clearly and concretely asserted in the Constitution, the Penal Code, the Civil Code, the Electoral Law, the Law on Military Service, the Law on Compulsory Education, the Law on Work, the Law on Autonomy of Ethnic Minority Regions, the General Disposal on Civil Law, etc. Tell them that no State organisation, social group, or in-dividual may compel a citizen to practise (or not practise) a religion, nor can any citizen be discriminated against because of his or her faith or absence of faith. They will shake their heads at your naive attitude,

and will think, if they don't say it, that all this is only "propaganda."

Anti-communism feeling is particularly strong in North America. In the United States, it started after the October Revolution of Russia in 1917 and played an increasing role in the foreign politics of this country. With the end of the Cold War and the disintegration of the USSR, the United States believed in the final victory of the Western democracy on socialism; however, the Cold War mentality has lasted until today. The fact that China, a country inspired and supported by communist spirit, succeeds so well while the American superpower appears to be running out of breath is a thorn in the side for the United States. It's also a huge contradiction for the empire of capitalism that dreamt of expanding its ideology on the world and imposing its values.

When the USSR took up capitalism, the United States needed another target, and they conjured up the "China threat." Washington continues with its containment measures and its engagements, offering both the carrot and the stick, in the hopes of changing China according to its own model. Therefore, human rights and democracy have become the major instruments for vilifying China every year, and it doesn't appear as though this strategy will abate in the new century.

Economic globalisation is the best channel to political globalisation. Washington takes the opportunity to promote its own values, such as freedom and democracy, and, as in a vicious circle, globalisation reinforces the United States arrogance and its will to push its ideological hegemony. On the other hand, the United States practises a politics of power, unlike China, and their tools are called Tibet, Taiwan, human

rights, and religious freedom.

In a *China Daily* article published in 1994, the author, a U.S. citizen, said that three kinds of people live in this world:

those who make events happen, those who watch the events happen, and those who don't even know that the events happen. Many United States citizens, because they have no interest in politics, don't see clearly the game their country is playing. A great number of them have never heard the expression "China threat" or "yellow peril" (the latter mostly used in French.). Propaganda is done both ways, but they ignore that.

Last time I went to Canada, my native country, I was interrogated for more than two hours, and my luggage searched in detail at the Vancouver airport. I didn't know then that Canadian Customs officials have no right to ask direct questions about religion and political party affiliation, and no right to search a traveller's luggage but they may ask the traveller to open this box, to show the contents of that bag. They are also allowed to ask indirect questions such as, "You work for a Chinese government's magazine?"; "China is a communist country, isn't it?"; and "So, you work for the communist party?" to exasperate you and provoke the "confession" that you are a communist, a bad communist.

For the Chinese, the word propaganda means "publicity." When they spread the idea of protecting the water and forests, they produce "propaganda." When they launch a product on the market or a writer's new book, it is "propaganda," they say. An information office is a propaganda bureau.

In the West, the anti-China feeling is so widely spread that it contaminates even the overseas Chinese. A Chinese woman, who emigrated to California when she was two, would liked to have fulfilled her husband's last wish and take his ashes back to China, but she was too afraid "to be thrown in the tomb and buried alive with him." What seems crass ignorance to us in China still leaves question marks in the minds of many Westerners to whom I like to tell this story only for the pleasure of seeing them wonder whether the Chinese widow was right. From there, one can easily graduate to stories of little girls being choked or drowned or cats being picked up in alleys to serve as dishes in restaurants, disguised as chicken, etc.

Some things that I find admirable in this country and that make life pleasant are seen in the West as big failures of the system, such as the re-education of criminals through labour, instead of seeing them play cards and watch TV as they do in some American prisons, at the expense of taxpayers (but people claim the injustice of the *laogai*, these reform-through-labour camps), and even the severity of punishment and capital punishment when there is reason and evidence (but this is called human rights abuse). Also, some countries, interfering in China's affairs, protect – after having received them as heroes – some Chinese dissidents and well-known criminals. The fact that dissidents exist is not surprising or dishonourable. They are a tiny minority among such a numerous population.

One should not believe that all the Chinese who emigrate are dissidents. What they look for is novelty, better material conditions, the possibility of using their talents to quickly earn money – impatient for their turn "because in China, there are too many people." Numerous in absolute numbers, they don't amount to much overall compared with those who stay voluntarily, because they have understood that the future is here. But those who are attracted by the overseas adventure may become prey to anti-China ideology, may be exploited by their adoptive country against their motherland, and without knowing it. This is how the United States offered immigrant status to 18,000 Chinese students who were there in 1989, under the pretext of "protecting them from the persecution" they would face if they returned to their country. On the other hand, the number of foreigners who live in China by choice and with pleasure and who are ready to do anything to remain here, and also those who became Chinese citizens when it still was possible is high.

Li Xiguang, a Chinese journalist who spent six months as an observer with the Washington Post in 1995, notes in an article that Dr. Zhu Weiyi from the Law School of Columbia University described the United States media as "launching a Cultural Revolution against China." The U.S. press took advantage of Harry Wu, who spread anti-China sentiment. But Wu himself was bested by the event. Wu Hongda was sent by China as a student to the United States for scientific research, but he failed totally. The best way to remain forever in the United States and take advantage of this country's money was to create a scandal against China.

Why did the United States turn him into an idol? Strangely enough, it seems that the United States trusts absolutely any immigrant who abandons his or her original name and cultural identity, adopts the U.S. culture, and stands against the motherland, even when this person has committed crimes against the United States by being there illegally. Too many foreign reports on China are simple and naive. When they talk about democracy (or its absence) in China, they prove that they have no knowledge of history at all. So they provoke hatred of China among their population and raise reasons for China to hate others.

Examples are not missing to an attentive eye, but are unseen by upstanding people, who are unconcerned and confident in the goodwill of Western democracy. Let's remember the distorted reports on Chinese orphanages, on the treatment of "political" prisoners, on the "cultural genocide" in Tibet, etc. Does the United States forget that it is one of the major sellers of weapons to other countries, despite the agreements signed and then denied, that half of the marriages celebrated in their nation end in divorce, that they have killed thousands of Iraqis by their sanctions, that they bombed the Chinese embassy in Yugoslavia where they were conducting a war of aggression, that racial discrimination is a major problem inside their frontier, that they have not paid their debt to the United Nations for years, and that they use double standards for judging "religious freedom" at home and in other countries?

Also, I would like to bring up my thoughts on two important points related to ideological propaganda: *Falun Gong* and Tibet.

Falun Gong, What is That?

I have so much to say about *Falun Gong* that I can't organise my thoughts properly. So, I will talk as if we were at a table, having lunch together.

In summer 2001, I spent one month in my homeland, Canada. Before going there, I intended to download information about *Falun Gong* from Internet, because the magazine I work for in Beijing often publishes articles about *Falun Gong*. My job is to translate from English into French, or polish articles translated from Chinese. How can I make sure I have the right words, if I don't read the original texts in French? In China, despite the fact that I'm a foreigner, I have to obey the rules as does any other citizen, and so I don't try to access *Falun Gong* sites on the Internet.

Why I Am Interested by Falun Gong

Since Falun Gong was prohibited in July 1999, and especially since the self-immolation of six persons by fire, on January 2001, on Tian'anmen Square, a lot of ink has covered the subject. I read all that was published in China about *Falun Gong*, and perhaps like many Chinese, I wondered if all what was being said by the authorities was completely right. Wouldn't they push to influence our thoughts a little? I was, and still am, against *Falun Gong*. But growing up in a Western society, I am used to making my own judgments after gathering my own information. I thought that even if only half of what was told here was true, it was enough to ban *Falun Gong,* but why not try to discover the truth about the other half, once I had the chance?

The First Time I Heard This Word

In 1989, before I came to China, I had a Chinese friend in Canada, whom I'll call Lao Z. Once, he thought he was catching a cold and told me, "When I go back home, I'll just practise *qigong* and my energy will be balanced. I'll be okay." It was the first time I had ever heard the word *qigong* and I asked him more about it. I thought it was interesting and worth a try, but he warned me, "*Qigong* may be dangerous if you don't have a genuine master to guide you." That's why, after I came to China, I made sure the master I chose was genuine and qualified. This masterÖ let's call him Lao W., told us students that *qigong* doesn't turn a sane person into a crazy one, but that it could introduce mental problems or instability if not practised correctly and under expert guidance. An example illustrates this: a woman in our class started to laugh and laugh, rolling on the ground as though possessed. Lao W. knew what to do and he helped her return to her normal state.

Our school of *qigong* was called "Nine rings" and it belongs to Taoism. I practised for over a year. The visible effects it had on me were that I lost a few extra kilos, I needed only three or four hours of sleep every night, I was never tired, and my mind was full of inspiration, exploding with ideas (which is good for a writer) after meditation. These were not my goal in the beginning; they happened as a matter of course.

Why I stopped practising has nothing to do with *qigong* itself. Later, I met Lao W. again, two or three times, with the others in the group. We found him to be absent-minded, closed, and strange. He didn't seem healthy. His wife asked us about him: what should we do now? Why was he acting as if she did not exist? No one could answer that. I called Lao W. at work. His colleagues said that he had quit the unit. Such a good job... something was surely going wrong. It's only when the words *Falun Gong* became common that I remembered he had told us once that, influenced by his brother, he had started to practise a new kind of *qigong*, and wanted to experience it before teaching it. So, *Falun Gong* had taken away a good friend, a very intelligent man, a husband, a good worker, and an honest citizen.

Meantime Lao Z., who had gone to Canada for one year in his field of work, decided to seek landed immigrant status. When he obtained it, he was joined by his two daughters and his wife, one by one. The whole family lived in miserable conditions in Montreal, as life is not easy for an artist, and not one of the four could speak any French or English. Six years later, Lao Z. came back to China for a visit. I saw him in his hometown in Shandong province. He told me he was astonished at how rapidly China had changed, and that he would not go back to Canada. His new plans were to wait for his second daughter to finish her studies in Canada (the mother and the older daughter were at that time working in a factory to allow her to study), and after that, they would all return to China.

Lao Z.'s wife had learned about *Falun Gong* in Canada. She told her husband how good it was, and he started to practise it in Jinan. Over a period of a year, he called me almost 10 times to invite me to "discover" *Falun Gong*. He gave me names and phone numbers of practitioners in Beijing, persons who would "instruct" me and give me Li Hongzhi's cassettes, etc. I am a naturally curious person. Normally, I would have gone to see what the big deal was. At that moment – maybe a guardian angel was protecting me – I felt no interest in this new discovery. Lao Z. told me that the kind of *qigong* I used to practise was not good, that his kind was the only one that could allow me "to meet my Creator after death." Finally, I had had enough and told him, "First, I have too much to do; I can't die. Second, I'm not sure that it's my priority to meet my Creator." After insisting on my conversion a few more times, he didn't bother me anymore.

Falun Gong *in Canada*

At the end of 2000 I saw Lao Z.'s name in a Canadian newspaper for which I write for. He had been arrested in China "for practising *Falun Gong*." Having kept his Chinese passport together with the Canadian one (which is illegal), he had been considered Chinese by the authorities, and the Canadian embassy had not obtained his release. I immediately asked the editor of that paper for the source of the news. He sent me the whole text. I read that Lao Z. had been arrested for a second time, and other details that showed that his arrest was not an abuse of process, but done according to Chinese law. Lao Z. had been practising *Falun Gong* in a public place, attracting spectators, and disturbing the public order. Being arrested twice meant, obviously, that he had done it more than once. It also showed that he had not been treated poorly the first time. I wrote an article about it in my weekly column of that paper. Following publication, I received e-mails and letters from readers who wanted to know more. I e-mailed them some articles we had published in China in our foreign languages magazines and invited them to read more on our Internet sites. They were very satisfied with the information, and none of them thought *Falun Gong* was good.

When I arrived in Montreal, I visited Chinatown. A few people – both Chinese and non-Chinese – were practising *Falun Gong*. They were also distributing papers. I took one. What was it? A 24-hour active appeal. "Canadian supporters condemn Jiang Zemin's brutal policy." The girl who had given me the paper had also said "Thank you" to me. I turned around and told her, "Why did you thank me? Don't imagine that taking your propaganda means that I support your group."

A few months before, my sister, who is a university professor, had copied notices for me, which had appeared in three universities of Montreal. They all invited people to attend their meetings and discover the "real nature" of *Falun Gong*. If just seen as a kind of relaxation exercise, *Falun Gong* is not bad. In most Western countries, people totally ignore it or place it in the same category as yoga, taiji, wushu, kongfu, and taekwondo.

In some bookstores in Canada, I asked for books about *Falun Gong*, just as a test. Out of five, three didn't know what I was talking about; one asked, "This is something Chinese, isn't it? A kind of a sect?" and the last one said, "No, we don't have any."

Why in China More Than in the West?

Why does *Falun Gong* proportionally harm more people in China than in the West? It's hard to explain unless one seriously researches the subject, and I don't think this has been done yet. Personally I think that it's because, in China, after the great efforts put into the war against Japan, the liberation of the country, and the founding of a New China, and involvement, willing or not, in the Cultural Revolution, the Chinese find themselves unsatisfied in a society that is far from perfect, and without a dream, an ambition, or an ideal. In the West, the regime is not perfect, either, but people have a wider choice of activities, sports, hobbies, and even religions or ideologies. They try everything but don't stick to a theory. In the last 20 years, studying esoteric matters, alternative medicine, or methods of relaxation has become fashionable, and there are so many schools that a person can easily ignore some. I asked a friend who teaches the history of religions what he thinks of *Falun Gong*. He said, "I can't say. It's only a minor sect, I have not yet started to pay attention to it."

From Montreal to Toronto

From Montreal, I went to Toronto. There, Chinatown is real! I also met two Chinese women who were distributing literature about *Falun Gong* and they were wearing a badge with the name of the sect. I asked them, first in English but quickly switching to Chinese, "Why are you here? If you really believe in *Falun Gong*, why don't you stay at home and practise it?" – "Because we want people to know the truth," one answered, while the other followed the conversation without opening her mouth. A long discussion started, and people, mostly Chinese, gathered around to see a *laowai* supporting China, which seemed strange to them, but they listened carefully. "What I don't like," I continued, "is that you mix politics with *Falun Gong*." The woman said they were not doing anything political. "If you can tell me that Jiang Zemin's name is not on these papers, I'll believe you." Of course, it was there! So, they *are* doing political things. *Falun Gong* people fight the Chinese government because their movement has been banned. They consider that such a decision is not justified and want to reverse it.

That woman was at Zhongnanhai on April 25, 1999, among the tens of thousands of *Falun Gong* practitioners who "peacefully disturbed" public order. Many of them have fled the country. Many, including others who had nothing to do with *Falun Gong* but just used the opportunity to emigrate, were welcomed by certain countries who also grabbed this opportunity to accuse China in the field of human rights. There were so many that, in the United States, immigration officials were requested to attend *Falun Gong* lectures to learn how to recognise false applications for a "refugee" status.

I told the woman, "You have started a political conflict, and you were given a political answer. You are a Chinese citizen. A citizen must obey the law. In China, no group manifestation is allowed without a permit, like it or not." She interrupted, "But we want to change that!" Accompanying me was a Chinese friend and her Canadian boyfriend, who is of Poland origin. He answered her, "Any government in the world would be afraid in front of a mass intervention." The woman said, "We know the government is frightened and we want to take advantage of it." I found this reaction childish. I added, "No one can change the world in one day. You have to be patient. Look how much progress China has made since the reform and opening-up policy started in the 1980s! Great achievements and remarkable changes have been accomplished in all fields. China accounts for one-fifth of the world population. It can't allow itself to make a mistake. The consequences would be too serious. Where do you think you're going by pushing the people into revolution, by encouraging turmoil? Just be patient. Things are moving and faster than you think. The law is the law. Anarchy will bring nothing good."

We talked for about an hour. I told her, finally, that I wanted to buy Li Hongzhi's books, to see what he said himself, not what other people have said about him or about *Falun Gong*. She congratulated me, saying that I was honest. She also thought that I could become a practitioner myself.

In fact, I had decided that, if after reading *Falun Dafa* or *Zhuan Falun*, I discovered that the State had lied, I would just shut up. Guess what I discovered? That it was true! It is the propaganda the movement distributes in the streets that contains unproven matters and other errors. For instance, Lao Z.'s photo was not him at all, and what is said about him is not true.

Falun Gong *in Books*

How can I become a practitioner by reading such a book as *Zhuan Falun*? Not only is it written poorly, the theory itself is a sloppy mixture of various ideologies – Buddhism,

Taoism, Islam, and Christianity. Li borrows from the sacred scriptures of these and more, but since few Chinese know about these four major sources, they think that Li Hongzhi has created a new theory. Moreover, they think he has been taught by... whom? Not the Buddha Sakyamuni, as "The level of Sakyamuni is that of a Tathagata (Buddha at the lowest level)," says the Master (p. 10). In fact, he created his theory: "I am the only person who is genuinely teaching *qigong* towards higher levels at home and abroad," he says (p. 1). Such a sentence is repeated continuously in the 10 lectures of the book. "Though some *qigong* masters have published some books, I am telling you that those books contain all kinds of things and are the same as what they practise, such as snakes, foxes, and yellow weasels. When one reads these books, these things will come out from the words. I have said that the number of fake *qigong* masters is many times more than that of genuine ones, and one cannot tell the difference." From these affirmations, which are used repeatedly, one can see, first, that Li Hongzhi wants to exercise absolute control over the minds of his disciples, and, second, that he has no respect for his disciples, whom he considers to have very little intelligence.

A slogan such as the *Falun Gong*'s, "Truth, Compassion, Tolerance" (Zhen-Shan-Ren) is not bad. In fact, it's attractive. But one can find these ideas elsewhere, as in the teachings of Jesus or Confucius. How can a sane person believe that the "Master" can "install a complete cultivation system in your bodies" (p. 6), a wheel that "is the miniature of the universe... that will forever rotate in your lower abdomen area" (p. 40). Or that "My Fashen (a body made of Gong and Fa) knows everything on your mind... before you think it." (p. 77). And this: "Once you want to truly practise cultivation, your life will be in danger instantly... I can do it (protect you) because I have numerous Fashen who possess my extraordinary divine powers and the powers of Fa.... Nobody will dare touch you. Besides, you have the protection of my Fashen, and you will not run into any danger" (p. 129). Follow several examples of persons who where not hurt by a car or didn't die in an accident "because I had the protection of Master Li" (p. 132), they believe. The Master's Fashen can also punish the practitioner who doesn't obey by "taking back every cultivation component installed in your body" (p. 84).

Falun Gong *and Health*

About health: a person "cannot practise cultivation with an ill body" (p. 2). The master can purify the body. Moreover, "your illnesses will be cured directly by me," he says (p. 123). Why, then, should a practitioner go to hospital, wait in line, and spend money? Li Hongzhi never said, at least in this one book, not to consult doctors or take medicine, but once he has full control of his disciples' minds, sentences like the former become, "I will not see a doctor for my stomach ache, just practise *Falun Gong*." But six months later, one patient was dead. He had cancer. Li didn't say medicine is not good; he just said that "80 to 90 percent of practitioners will become free of illnesses" (p. 222). Li spoke so much of that wheel of law that he installed in each practitioner that an "illuminated" one opened his abdomen with a knife to see it! Li said he could protect his disciples anywhere and against any danger. Why not to try to fly from the 9th floor? The powerful Master Li can do all sorts of things! "I have removed *Futi* (spirit possession) from the bodies of genuine practitioners, removed all such bad things from the inside to the outside of your bodies... eliminated demons. I will also clean up your body.... I can do that... I can do it only for practitioners... The master possesses great energy potency, he can eliminate your karma" (pp. 125, 127).

Li also teaches that each body contains "the white substance and the black substance" (p. 140). A person gains or loses the black substance according to deeds, bad or good, that he or she commits. The five victims of fire immolation in January 2001 thought they had accumulated enough "white substance" to leave this world without suffering but they saw how much "black substance" was still in their bodies and understood that they had been cheated.

Not only is Li Hongzhi's theory ridiculous, the principles upon which it is based are the most elementary science, things that a first-grade pupil knows (pp. 18, 164, 267). Don't be jealous, be detached, right your mind, dominate yourself, be even-tempered – all these healthy habits don't need Master Li to discover them. If Li forbids his cult members to read other books except those he wrote himself, it may be to not let them discover where he borrowed his theory. Actually, absolutely nothing is new in what he preaches.

About how to study *Falun Gong*, Li says, "by reading my book, watching my video tapes, or listening to my recording" and "There is only one master of Dafa.... Therefore, nobody else is able to teach this Fa" (p. 136). How did *Falun Gong* gain so many followers in 8 and 10 years? What is so appealing in having your mind fully controlled by another person? I think the *Falun Gong* method for recruiting members is simple. Recruitment is done by friends, family members, and colleagues. People join a group that offers truthfulness, benevolence, and tolerance, – what everyone should cultivate – and a group that promises to fulfil their human and natural needs.

Conclusion

Li warned his practitioners that practising *qigong* may be dangerous. One could become mentally unbalanced, and it would be disastrous for *Falun Gong*'s reputation. He thinks that a problem occurs "when a person's Zhu Yishi (main consciousness) becomes too weak.... He always remains in trance and cannot lift up his spirit" (p. 209). Easy to say! Li divides the "ordinary persons" from the "genuine practitioners," as he speaks of "the other *qigong* masters" and "himself, the only true one." But he forgets that his practitioners are all "ordinary persons" before becoming "Buddhas." It's easy to misunderstand what is said, to interpret subjectively, to have such a high ideal that one becomes mental unstable, insane, or even commits suicide in desperation. Enlightenment is not for everyone in this world. This is the big mistake Li has made, letting the masses think that they all could reach it. To date, over 1,600 persons have been victims of Master Li.

Today, China has almost put an end to *Falun Gong* in its territory. Intervention workshops help *Falun Gong* members give up the cult and go back to their families, their work, and their normal lives. And it is about time.

The Real Problem

In the history of international relations, Tibet is a political stake and the Dalai Lama, a pawn on the chessboard. Most of the persons interested in Tibet I know, from any country tourists are full of prejudices about "the roof of the world." I must say they are also honest, and if they seek for truth when they visit Tibet, we may expect their opinion to change, for how brilliant reality is, when one sees it with his or her own eyes. Still too many persons ignore the culture and history of

Tibet; as they can't communicate directly in Chinese or Tibetan with the local people, they are satisfied with what, through the objective of their camera, confirm their prejudices. What a deception, when I go abroad and give a lecture about Tibet, followed by a question period! The questions usually show that listeners don't keep what goes against their prejudices, but hear only what they want to hear and what doesn't disturb their "Tibetan imaginary." Here is an example. A Canadian friend of mine, a university professor, went to Tibet in May 1997. Later, he told me that he and his group had been sent away from a Tibetan restaurant by the police, and were obliged to go to a Chinese establishment. The reason was, according to his judgement, racism, an attempt to "break" the Tibetan nation. This was his immediate analysis,

without understanding a word of what was going on, based only on prejudice. I myself don't know the reason since I was not there, but after discussing this with Chinese persons, including Tibetans, we all concluded that his offered reason was unlikely, and that the real cause might have been one or more of the following: the owner of the Tibetan restaurant had no permit; he had not paid his taxes; the place was not hygienic enough for foreigners; the owner and the policeman had a personal dispute; the owner was trafficking ancient *tanka*, etc.

Tibetans Outside of Tibet

Here, I would like to underline the major difference I found between the Tibetans in Tibet or in Xiahe (Gansu Province), and the Tibetans who live in Nepal. The former don't discuss politics and don't seem interested in it. They live happily and quietly, and, except for a handful of "separatist" monks I met in Lhasa, the ordinary citizens don't mind who governs, as long as they continue to develop year after year.

In the Tibetan village of Tashiling, on the outskirts of Pokara (Nepal), my husband and I spent two hours chatting with the women at the market, while waiting for the rain to stop. The major difference between them and the Tibetans of China is that they all think according to the same and unique pattern: the bad Chinese invaded Tibet and forced them to flee the country. "When our country is free," said one woman, "we'll go back immediately and get a good job! Do you think this is a life, what we do here? Commerce!"

I took pity on her, not because she had a miserable life (indeed, I don't think any of them do), but because she was so narrow-minded by anti-China propaganda. I told her that all the Tibetans I met before knew very well everything that the central government of China had done for them. They appreciate it and don't seek independence. "I'm sorry to tell you," I said, "that you fool yourself if you think that your

Tibetan fellows inside the country are thinking the same way you do and support your efforts for independence. Instead, I know Hans, too, who live in Tibet, and they don't want to leave because they think the real life, the real freedom, the real peace is there, in Tibet. If your 'country' were free, it would not take long before another powerful country takes a bite of it; and you would flee again. Where? Towards east, this time, to China!"

She stared at me, her eyes wide open. "Have you ever been to Tibet?"

"Of course! If not, how could we speak like this? My husband also has been there two months last year and is going again for another month when we leave Nepal." Then, she asked me when I had been in Tibet, and was disappointed to hear I was not there on the 10th of March.

"Which year?" I asked.

"Every year! Every year on March 10, the Tibetans of the world march for independence. If you go to Tibet on that day, you'll see the Chinese army killing so many people in the streets."

Wow! I felt as though I had been transported to another planet! "How do you know that, if you have never been in Tibet?"

"We have seen photos, and videos. Every year we see them."

"Who took these photos?"

"Foreigners. From Taiwan, and other places."

I asked her why they had chosen March 10 but she could not answer. I, a Canadian living in China, had to explain to her that on March 10, 1959, the Dalai Lama and his supporters had torn up the "17 Articles Agreement," which had initiated an armed rebellion in Lhasa.

Now. Let us use our brains for a moment. First, if what she said were true, would the Chinese authorities let foreigners film the "show"? Second, Tibet is not only one people, only one nation, but several ethnic branches, and civil wars and disorders have been common on its territory. During the Cultural Revolution, Tibetans, just as other Chinese, have suffered and been treated badly. Tibetan Red Guards were very active among their own people, some of them told me. Therefore it is realistic to expect that several persons were killed, and that photos had been taken.

"Are you sure these photos and films were taken recently, on March the 10th each year? Might you not have been deceived? Maybe they show you the same pictures year after year? Maybe the photos were altered?"

She, as the interpreter of the others around, said, "It's possible, but we have no means of checking."

"Might these activist friends of the Dalai Lama," I continued, "be the authors of the photocopied letters on the board at the village entrance, issued by 'His Holiness Dalai Lama's office? And the inscription 'Chinese, leave', who do you think wrote it?"

Then my husband and I explained to them all the changes that had happened in Tibet, especially under the reform and opening-up policy, all the money invested into reconstruction and development by the central government, the progress in education, the religious freedom, the improvement of health, society, life, etc. They were astonished! Apparently, no one had ever spoken to them like this.

"Do you believe me?" I asked.

"I believe you because you are a foreigner," said the woman. "And I believe you," she said to my husband, who is Chinese, "because you're not a member of the communist party. Are you?"

"You can trust us, my friends," I added, "we tell you only what we have seen. Tibet is a beautiful and peaceful place where people sing while they work, where people smile and enjoy life."

In fact, one woman was talking for the group because she could speak *putonghua* while the others around could follow the conversation through her translation, and agreed. The younger ones among them were born in Nepal; others had fled Tibet to go to Nepal in the 1950s and never returned. They have no passports, so of course they can't enter Tibet! China is like any other country in the world: no illegal visitors!

We then visited a temple where a young 17-year-old monk said that his greatest aspiration was to see Tibet but that he could not go unless he was disguised, which he meant, "After my hair has grown longer to hide the fact that I am a monk, because the monks," he explained, "are arrested and jailed or even killed."

"How do you know that?" I asked, showing interest in his revelation.

"A friend of mine left here and never came back!"

"I'll tell you something, young man. Your friend may have been arrested because he entered a country illegally. But if you never heard from him after that, don't you think he might have accomplished his great desire: to see Tibet? He may be living in a monastery there!"

He bowed his head and said, "I wish I had such a chance!"

Finally, I realised that the Tibetans outside of Tibet are the victims not only of ignorance but of a well-organised campaign of misinformation. And I went on thinking that the Dalai Lama, in fact, who left the country when he was still so young and under the influence of a clique, and never saw

Tibet with his own eyes after coming to the age he could judge by himself, is also a poor victim. A puppet.

Variety of Chinese Culture

Art of Tea

Everywhere in China, people drink tea, even though the tea plant doesn't grow all over the country. Its preparation is an art; more than a way to quench the thirst; tea that is drunk by friends plays a sentimental and social role.

In China, more than 600 varieties of tea are known. Generally, the one called "red tea" is the one that the West calls "black tea," referring to the colour of its leaves in the package, while China refers to the colour of the infusion.

Green tea offers an unlimited scale of the product: dark and bitter in Hunan, clear and light in Zhejiang, such as the Dragon Well or Longjing tea, which is very bitter and with a medicinal taste in some areas of Yunnan. Yet the first harvest must be distinguished from the second and the third, as well as the size of the leaves and their position on the branch. The very tiny tipped leaves don't taste the same as the large ones that grow in the shadow of others.

Hua cha or *molihua*, jasmine-scented tea, is very popular, and it's what laypeople call "Chinese tea." *Juhua cha* is not tea, in fact, but an infusion of chrysanthemum flowers, and it is generally drunk with sugar, crystallised, in big pieces and not refined; it melts slowly at the bottom of the cup.

If there are inexpensive teas, there are also fancy ones that cost up to 1,500 or 2,000 yuan for 500 grams (US$181-242).

Not only do prices vary, but the aspect of the leaves: for instance, some leaves seem to be rolled up on themselves, like an insect larva starting a cocoon. This is the case of the Anhui Province's *qi men hong* tea. The *qian li xiang* (tea that can be smelled from 1,000 *li*) comes in little balls that will blossom in the water. It is thus called "pearl tea." Sometimes, the leaves seem to have been minced or crushed. Sometimes they are flat and complete, like the *longjing cha.* Mongols and Tibetans consume brick tea; this means that the leaves have been pressed into a loaf before drying. They break a piece of the "brick" to prepare tea, but it is not enough to pour water on the leaves; the tea must boil. Then yak butter is added to the infusion, as well as salt or sugar, depending on the region. Hui people (Muslims who live mostly in Ningxia) serve *ba bao cha* (8-treasures tea). Besides green tea leaves, this delicious drink contains *gouqi* (wolfberries), dried fruit, walnuts, sesame seeds, raisins, *zao* (Chinese dates), *longan* or "dragon eyes," sugar or honey, and, sometimes, even a spoonful of rose or osmanthus flower jam.

Tea must not be infused with boiling water, but with water that has boiled and is still very hot. This is especially true for young teas. Boiling water would burn the leaves, and their perfume would not be released.

The stronger the tea, the more water can be added to the same leaves without changing or adding more. Some persons throw away the first infusion, saying that it's best just "to wash the leaves." This is done especially with a bitter tea. Generally, the second and the third infusions are best.

Some teas, on the contrary, are soon "exhausted," such

as the *tie guan yin*, a high-quality tea with a delicate aroma, or the white tea, which don't have any taste after the second infusion.

It is said that tea should never remain steeped overnight, because if the leaves remain too long without new water being added, they release an acidity that squanders the taste.

I could talk at length about teapots, tea bowls, and other accessories that, in fact, play a small role in the preparation of an excellent tea, but I will limit myself to saying that if one starts consuming tea directly from a small clay teapot chosen carefully, drinking from the spout, ensuring that it fills and fits the hand comfortably and that its shape is pleasing to the eye, one would never again drink tea from a glass or a cup.

Clay teapots retain the taste of tea, because the dregs cling and form a crust. Naturally, a teapot must not be washed with detergent, which would destroy the taste, and the crust, patiently formed over time, must not be removed. It makes all the difference in a new piece of crockery and a personal selection. I myself have several teapots, each for a typical kind of tea, but also for a special place: one in the living room, one in the office, and even one in Canada, which waits for me on my holidays.

There are tea sets so small that they seem like toys. Some sets offer for each guest a little bowl, wider than its height, and a goblet, taller than its width, and of a diameter smaller than the bowl's. In this case, the tea is poured in the bowl, and the goblet serves as a lid. After a few minutes, the scented steam has been stored in the "cover" and the drinker may inhale it, a double pleasure: olfactory and gustatory.

Is there anything more disgusting and undrinkable than the tea from a teabag served in a plastic glass, or worse, a paper cup? Moreover, the teabags sold in America or Europe contain too many leaves for one cup. Some persons then soak the bag in the water a few seconds and throw it away before the infusion becomes too strong. In doing so, they drink only the bitterness of the leaves, while the true flavour ends up in the garbage.

Lemon tea, iced and sweetened, is another Western invention that recently entered China. But the Chinese invented a carbonated tea soft drink, delicious and refreshing, with guaranteed success, I think. Also, if the Chinese take tea anywhere and at anytime, they usually don't have tea during meals, but this habit may be about to change, perhaps under the influence of foreigners in China.

Except in tourist areas, restaurants that have seen very few foreigners often don't have a single tea leaf in the establishment. I have seen a restaurant owner sending her daughter home for some to satisfy three Westerners and, recently, a waitress offered to share her own jar with a customer who absolutely wanted to drink tea.

In the beginning, tea was the beverage of Buddhist and Taoist monks who used it to stay awake during their martial arts exercises. Through history, tea has occupied its place in medicine, art, religion, poetry, and has become a symbol of respect (such as the daughter-in-law offering some to her future mother-in-law,) of friendship, and of harmony (it is taken between friends in tiny cups).

The art of preparing tea has been known for at least 4,000 years (6,000 according to certain authors). One places the leaves in a porcelain or clay teapot, and then turns the teapot to wet them. Once the aroma is noticeable, the teapot can be filled. After a few minutes, when all the leaves have settled, the infusion is ready.

In Fujian Province, the famous *wulong* (or *oolong*) tea

requires its own preparation called *gongfu cha*. The infusion is made very strong; the outside of the teapot is generously watered after the lid is placed on it. The first infusion is said to wash the leaves as well as the goblets. The little 10 ml cups are placed in a row or in a circle. Instead of completely filling the first one, then the second, and so on, the host pours the tea in a circular and continuing movement, so that each guest gets the same strength and the same colour, as a sign of friendship and honesty.

There are some interesting legends around tea, one of which is about the *biluochun*. This green tea has been produced in Suzhou, Jiangsu Province for 1,000 years. The shell shape of the leaves comes from a special manipulation during the drying procedure, which is at 120 degrees Celsius for 8 minutes. The leaves dance in the glass like petals of flowers on the water, revealing a nice tender green and a lightly sweet flavour.

It is said that the best *biluochun* is picked by the mouths of young girls who then place it at their breasts where it dries from the heat of their bodies. The legend refers to the beautiful Biluo, of the Tang dynasty, whose fiancÈ had been wounded by a dragon far away. The only way to save him was revealed to the young woman in a dream: she should take the leaves of a special plant and infuse them. But, it was winter, and the tree was covered with snow. Biluo had to keep the twig in her mouth till the buds bloomed. She saved her fiancÈ, but perished from the cold. In the spring, thousands of little plants sprouted around her tomb.

The *biluochun* tea (*chun* means "spring") is gathered in March. An expert may pick half a kilo a day, which translates into 150 grams of finished tea. Drying doesn't suffer waiting, because the leaves could easily turn yellow. Including the process of shells preparation (8 minutes), 35 minutes are needed for drying, a few grams at a time, plus 15 for cooling. It's easy to imagine the price of this tea!

Pearls: Jewels and Medicines

In southeastern Zhejiang province one can find the greatest pearl markets not only in China but in the world. The names Wenling and Zhuji, for example, are well-known in the field, as well as the Shanxiahu (lake under the mountain) market. Every day buyers arrive from all over the country, and the business revenue is astronomical.

Most of the local pearls are cultivated in fresh water. The shells are suspended by a string, which is held by a floating bamboo stick for more than a year before the pearls are ready for the market.

In Beijing, also, one can buy pearls. They all come from Zhejiang. On the 3rd floor of the Hongqiao Market, in the capital, the sellers can be heard calling each other from their respective stands in their local dialect. The one who has served me since I came to China, Mr. Li, has become a friend. He taught me a lot about pearls.

First, real pearls are always cold, while the false ones acclimate to the weather. Pearls grow rapidly in the first eight months, but the following years will see them grow a millimetre a year. That's why small pearls or young pearls cost much less than the bigger ones. Only an experienced eye can see the difference of age – and of price, then – between two pearls. Some customers may ask which are "the best quality" pearls: the shiny ones, the translucent, or the milky ones. These characteristics have nothing to do with the quality. One chooses according to his or her taste. Moreover, buying pearls at gross market price, a person may have some of all kinds and colours. But be careful: the natural colours of the pearls cover the whole range of whites, pinks, and greys. Purple, gold, green, or yellow pearls are laser-dyed. In fact, the pearl itself is natural, but the colour is not.

A difference exists also between the fresh-water pearls and the sea-water pearls, and it's not in the round or the irregular shape, but mostly in weight and fragility.

A pearl is cultivated from a grain of sand or stone placed in the shell to force the oyster to coat it so that it won't get scratched. If the sand is a big grain, the pearl begins with an advantage of size. In the end, the pearl will contain much sand and little coating, and be heavier and more resistant than the sea pearl, which is made from fine sand. If the coating is thicker, it is also more fragile.

The best quality pearls are the biggest, of course, perfectly round and with light nuances of pink. They are used to make necklaces or decorate jewellery. Smaller and irregular pearls are reduced in powder for pharmaceutical or cosmetic use.

Pearl powder has been used in medicine for 2,000 years. It contains several amino acids, has sedative and nutritional value, and is effective in the treatment of high-blood pressure and minor heart ailments. Its treatment is gentle and doesn't have side effects. A few years ago, science succeeded in making it completely soluble in water. Its absorption by the body is then complete.

Powdered pearls are also used in some cosmetics; they are said to keep people youthful and prevent wrinkles. Such cosmetics are appreciated by the stars of the large and small screens.

The powder is obtained after the pearls have been sterilised in boiling water and crushed for 120 hours! The whole process requires care and attention. First, only absolutely pure pearls are chosen. Then, the powder is saved in porcelain or glass capsules to keep its purity and beneficial quality.

On January 1, 1992, Zhejiang Province authorised the free sale of pearl powder. On the one hand, as the product was then worth US$110 per kilogram, unscrupulous entrepreneurs appeared. Some manufacturers have been caught mixing mother of pearl with the pearl powder. Experts may detect fraud by the smell and the multicoloured spectrum that appears under solar light.

On the other hand, some pearls are first selected for necklaces and rejected later. These pearls are bathed in melted wax, which helps making their colour uniform; some wax may remain and combine with the pearl material. Others, when they are discarded, have already been pierced to hold a string. In this case, the hole may contain iron left by the drill, and these pearls are dangerous when developed for internal use. Impure pearls may be sorted by magnets, which attract their iron particles, which are invisible to human eye.

The Marvellous Arts of Paper

Papercut

If Canadians make an art of tearing paper, and the Japanese of folding paper (origami), the Chinese have cut paper. Paper cuts are a popular art created, obviously, from paper and other thin material, by using scissors or an etching needle. The silver sheet decoration of the Warring States Period found in Gutu Village, in Hunan Province, and the gold sheet decoration of the Han period discovered in Xinjiang also belong to the art of paper cutting.

Where does this art come from? The legend says that Emperor Hui of the Jin offered a banquet during the first month of the lunar year. Since there were no flowers, he ordered young girls to cut out flower patterns of five colours.

In the beginning, paper cuts also were used to decorate clothes and as embroidery patterns. During the Tang Dynasty, paper cuts were offered as gifts. They represented "beauties" (famous beautiful women), flowers, birds, trees, and insects.

Paper cut styles vary according to region, culture, habits, living conditions, and geographic and ethnic environment. In the south, those of Guangdong Province and especially of Foshan, are very fine and particularly expressive. Those engraved in Yueqing, Zhejiang Province, are renowned for the beautifully clear, fine style.

On the loess plateau in Shaanxi Province the tradition has been better preserved. In Ansai, 19,000 women's scissors give birth every day to vividly coloured birds, imaginary butterflies, flowers from another world, rainbow-tailed fishes, the 12 animals of the zodiac, Peking Opera masks, and many other fantasies. About 100 of them are considered as exceptionally talented artists.

A woman in her 80s, seeing her end near, gave her daughter-in-law the patterns she had created and said, "I have nothing else to leave to this world. Now, I can go in peace. My work will not have been lost."

Ansai girls learn to cut paper at a young age. Knowing how to make paper cuts is a measure of refinement and often a straightforward measure of a woman's worth in Ansai. Paper cutting is associated with embroidery, and the artisans often practise both.

Cutting may be done in hollows or in relief. That means

the figure, bird or flower is cut away, and what remains is its silhouette; or the object of the cutting is what is kept, and it is evidenced by the blank created around it. Some works in burnt motives are accomplished with incense or charcoal, or engraved with an etching needle; others are made from hand-torn paper.

Such an art pervades each moment of life. Nice drawings decorate ceilings, doors, and windows for traditional festivities, and create a joyous and lively ambience. At weddings, paper cuts decorate the nuptial room as well as the whole house and the reception room. They are present at funerals as well. Moreover, this art is used in architecture, wood sculptures, porcelain decorations; in modern life, we find it in store decorations, book covers and illustrations, postage stamps, etc.

There are some very small pieces as well as immense cuttings. Some works are made of monochrome red or black paper; others are white. In this case, the cuttings will be painted and become multi-hued. The paper being very thin, many layers are cut at the same time. Some artists prefer to draw a model first; others just follow the inspiration of their scissors. A woman from Pingyao, in Shanxi, told me, "My scissors lead me; I never know where they will bring me."

The most common papers cuts, often sold in bundles of eight or ten, are 7 cm by 10, more or less. They are easy to slide in an envelope with a greeting letter. I am always surprised to see the effect they produce on my friends abroad; they never leave them indifferent. Some people will pay a lot to frame them, enhancing their value.

The art of paper cutting in Ansai is a story of 7,000 years of history, aesthetic, civilisation, and anthropology.

The Dancing Dragon

Paper articles that enhance the atmosphere of great national festivities are of two kinds: entertaining, such as the lion or dragon that serve for a dance, kites, lanterns, and models of boats; and sacred, as in religious rites – deities, buddhas, demons, and paper-made persons and horses.

The dragon is a fabulous animal that has inhabited the Chinese people's imagination for millennia. The dancing dragon seen in festivities has a bamboo or metallic wire skeleton wrapped in construction paper. Three-year-old bamboo must be cut in the 9th lunar month because in this period, their water content is low and they are flexible enough to be stretched and folded. Before preparing the structure, bamboos are peeled and cut in several strips, submitted to an antiseptic and pesticide treatment, and each strip is coated with paper.

The paper covering the outside is cut in strips and twisted. The process continues step by step: the stiffening precedes pasting; sunken parts go before convex parts; the maker goes from dark to light, from the back to the middle, from the inside to the outside. The dragon is then painted with vivid colours. Its features are generally exaggerated, its mouth half-open. The tongue may be mobile, and usually a pearl is ensconced between its teeth. With long, flossy beards and large, round eyes, the dragon has an impressive bearing. The beast seems immense and densely alive, but, in fact, it's less than 3 kg. The handlers now only have to learn how to make it move naturally and easily.

The *"Xuan"* Paper

The making of paper is a great contribution of the Chinese people to world civilisation. China already used ramie, hemp, and flax fibre to make paper at the beginning of the

Western Han Dynasty, in the 3rd century.

The Baqiao paper, discovered in August 1957 in an ancient tomb of Xi'an suburb, is the oldest fibrous paper in the world.

Paper made under Cai Lun's supervision, in the Eastern Han period, was used for writing and its quality improved constantly through the centuries. Calligraphy and Chinese painting are products of the *xuan* paper, or Xuancheng, in the Jing District, Anhui Province.

At the end of the Song Dynasty, fleeing from continuous civil wars, Chao Dasan arrived in Xuancheng, a region of sandalwood and crystal waters. He settled down and made paper. Even now, the makers of *xuan* paper are the Chao family.

The raw material consists in sandalwood bark and rice straw. The straw, dried on the hills, undergoes a soaking in water, then, in lime, followed by packing, fermentation, steam cooking, drying, and bleaching in the sun. Then, workers proceed to washing, sorting out the raw material, cutting, and preparing pulp.

The *xuan* paper quality and thickness uniformity rely on the artisan's technique, on the raw material, and the water quality. The sandalwood bark features a fine and resistant fibre, of homogenous length and size; that's why the Xuancheng paper obtained by filtering is flexible. Local waters are clean and clear; consequently, the paper is immaculately white.

Drying on a low fire consists in taking out the sheets of paper from the water, one by one, and sticking them on the heated wall. When it is dry, the paper peels off easily.

Xuan paper may be divided into three categories according to the proportion of raw materials used: neat sandalwood bark, crude bark, and rice straw. The first one suits painting; the third one, being supple, suits calligraphy. In a phrase, Xuancheng paper is thin, flexible, clean, and white. It never yellows and resists insects and mould. Consequently, it also suits official and historical documents. When one buys artwork on *xuan* paper, the seller folds and refolds it, and even presses the folds before giving it to the buyer. This seemed scandalous to me, at first, but I soon realised that *xuan* paper resists permanent folds. When mounted, all the temporary folds disappear without difficulty.

In mounting calligraphy and paintings, in principle, one-third of the surface is given to the work itself and two-thirds to the frame. As calligraphy and Chinese paintings are usually made on *xuan* paper, which is very thin the work must be mounted by a master to avoid warping and shrinking. The mounting technique of silk or paper artwork is an art in itself.

Puppets and Statuettes

Puppets come in a vast range: with strings, with sheaths, or are manipulated by horizontal sticks of bamboo. Another form of this type of culture is the shadow theatre. Besides the puppets, characters and animals are represented in three dimensional figurines, the most famous being the painted clay figures of Tianjin; the figures of Huishan, and others made of blown sugar, as in blown glass, and flour dough; and the dolls in national costumes, which are sometimes so tiny and fragile that they are kept under a globe; the characters on horsehair bases of Beijing; and, finally, the wood-carved puppets.

String Puppets

Quanzhou, an old city of Fujian Province, is famous for

its puppet theatre. Each puppet is controlled by 20 or 30 strings, which are linked to a board that the handlers hold. If the strings are the nerves of the puppets, this board is then a knot of nerves. Quanzhou puppet theatre has something unique: it is accompanied by special music – the *kuilei qiang* or puppet melody. The operator, whose hands are occupied, must also beat the drum with the foot. In order to make the puppet move naturally, the puppeteer uses all the muscles of the hands and fingers.

Inside the string puppets are braided bamboo or cane lashes. In Quanzhou, their heads are carved and painted camphor wood.

Sheath Puppets

These puppets are placed on the hands like a glove. The palm is used as the body, the forefinger supports the head, the thumb on one side and the other fingers supporting the arms, which is challenging since the puppeteer must maintain an angle of 90 degrees between the forefinger and the middle finger. Each finger must be able to move independently.

This art is ancient, since in the Mogao caves in Dunhuang (Gansu), on a fresco painted under the Tang, one can see a woman handling a puppet to amuse the children around her.

Like its stringed sister, the sheath puppet has a camphor wood head and comes from south Fujian. The rich costumes, often embroidered, are made with care and refinement, which make the puppets real artwork.

Shadow Puppets

This kind of theatre dates back more than one millennium. Under the Yuan, when wars were raging, theatre companies followed the armies; they thus needed light and handy accessories. Characters, animals, accessories and stage settings were cut out from the hind quarters of donkey, sheep or ox skin and become translucent after being soaked, scraped, and dried.

Today, in the north, donkey skin is what is used mainly, for its flexibility, making it possible for the figures to swivel or tumble elegantly.

According to the method of sculpture, we obtain either a face by keeping the skin and rejecting the line, or the reverse, that is an perforated product. The characters are two-dimensional, and flat; the heads are generally traced of profile, and dismountable. A hundred bodies can match three or four heads.

This art continues to evolve. The figures of the contemporary shadow theatre may have celluloid and mobile eyes; the mouth may open and close.

Half a century ago, soy oil lamps with seven wicks were used as lighting; then, gas lamps. Today, fluorescent tubes don't allow the spectators to see the shades of the stalks on the screen.

A skilful manipulator can play with 15 stalks simultaneously. The shadow theatre has a 6-m length screen; the height of the characters varies from 20 to 60 cm.

Huishan Clay Figurines

The Jiangsu black clay comes from an underground layer at the foot of Mount Beipo. Approximately only one hectare remains. It is fine, smooth, flexible, scratch resistant, and it dries without cracking.

Appeared during the Ming Dynasty, the Huishan clay figurines have nearly 500 years of history. They are produced from a mould, or entirely hand modelled, which gives a more refined product. They represent the life of the people, and often have animals and children as a subject. Around 1870, production of dramatic characters started, inspired by Peking Opera figures, *kunqu* (traditional opera of Jiangsu), myths, customs, and traditions.

Their production requires 18 processes, including modelling, kneading, choosing, beating, cutting, pressing, gluing, incrustation, polishing, scraping, cleaning, varnishing, and decorating. They are not baked in the oven; rather, they dry in the shade and painted in an established order: top to bottom, pale to dark, white to black, ending with the hair and shoulders. Some colours can require four layers.

They are appreciated not only for their visual aesthetics, but because they reflect the charm of life in the south of Yangtze River.

Figures on Horsehair Bases

Specifically, these are "horsehair bases" – not made from horsehair. The *zong ren* is a craft product of Beijing. This small character, which appeared only 100 hundred years ago, takes its origin from traditional opera and is inspired from folklore.

The horsehair is fixed to the clay base of the character. Of flexible material and cut at various angles, the hair allows the character, which is placed on a copper plate that one strikes with the hand, to turn in either direction. The *zong ren* can fight, collide, and jump, but will never fall.

The primitive *zong ren* were made of multicoloured paper, sorghum stalk, and clay. Now, they are dressed of cotton, measure from 8 to 20 cm and are extremely refined.

The head is made of clay, with the face painted like Peking Opera characters. Arms are made of a wire passing through the sorghum stalk and then stuffed with cotton. The legs are made in the same way; the characters formerly were tubular and had no legs.

Embroidery and Brocade

The four famous types of Chinese embroidery are those of Suzhou, Sichuan, Guangdong, and Hunan. The latter dates back more than 2,000 years. On some pieces that have been found in old tombs are refined and natural stitches, and distinguished drawings.

The "Xiangxiu embroidery" resorts to a system of disordered stitches and Jacquard. Polychrome threads are used, all in nuances of a colour, to produce chiaroscuro and a realistic effect.

The production includes embroidered portraits of historical characters; animals, such as a lion or a tiger, with a "relief" effect obtained by the hidden thread in the fabric; a peacock, with dishevelled stitches, giving a velvety impression of feathers; the double-face embroidery, which offers on one side a winter landscape, and on the other, a summer landscape; and perfectly identical images on both sides in drawing, colour, and dimension, a superb work in which art exceeds nature. If the single face embroidery can allow threads and knots to show, the double-face style must hide them absolutely.

The embroidery with hair goes back one millennium at least. We are not short of yet another legendÖ Under the Song Dynasty, a girl copied the lotus sutra with her blood in order to obtain longevity for her mother. Then, to express her sincerity to Buddha, she embroidered tens of thousands of characters with her hair, marrying her piety to her art.

This type of embroidery is called "ink embroidery" because black and white are the main hair colours of the

Chinese, but today, the whole range of hair colour is used: blond, red, auburn, which makes polychrome images possible.

Human hair passes strict standards and complicated treatments before being used for embroidery. It has to be softened, degreased, and sometimes dyed. Colours difficult to find or not existing in nature are manufactured. Human hair particularly suits the reproduction of furry animals.

China was a pioneer in raising silk worms 5,000 years ago. Among the many results of the work of silk are brocade, gauze, satin, crepe, down, velvet, coarse-grained silk, each as splendid as the other.

Brocade is a multi-layer fabric woven with at least two kinds of polychrome threads on a special Jacquard loom. It results both from the weaving method and from the chain and screen colour. This is why brocade is thick and heavy. Initially, the image is outlined and then machine-pressed before the weaving. The Chinese character "*jin*," which contains the root of "gold," indicates brocade, that is, it's worth its weight in gold.

The history of Chinese brocade met three high levels: Shujin of Sichuan, Songjin of Suzhou, and Yunjin of Nanjing. Hangzhou's brocade takes after the simplicity of the first and the refinement of the second, as well as the local landscape. Around 1920 Du Jinsheng, who left his name to the product, started to boldly weave mounts and waterscapes after having worked for a long time on "The West Lake." Currently, the Dujinsheng brocade offers black and white or multi-coloured weavings.

Cloisonné

One of China's "four technologies," it dates back to the

Jingtai emperor of the Ming Dynasty, the reason for its designation being *jingtailan*. In the golden age of cloisonné, several varnishes were used, among which blue was the fundamental base (*lan* means "blue").

The manufacturing includes making the shape, filigreeing, enamelling, cooking, polishing, and gilding. The base shape is made of copper, and its thickness must be uniform. The contour must be smooth, without scratches due to filing, or hollows.

Then, according to the lines of the model, which is copied with carbon paper, the artisan works a thin copper wire with tweezers, folding it or rolling it up at will, obtaining a stereoscopic image, which is then welded on the copper base.

After a wash with acid, enamelling fills all the vacuums with powders of various colours, as a painter chooses colours and nuances that will offer perspective and movement. During cooking at maximum temperature, the powder will liquefy and turn into its real colour.

Once cooled, the piece will be polished with materials such as emery, topaz, and charcoal. The well-furbished work will have a fine, smooth, and uniform surface. At last, gilding, with a very fine brush, will emphasise beauty and elegance. All of the above are done by hand.

Red Clay and Black Clay

Red Clay Teapots

When Su Dongpo taught in Yixing, a teapot with a handle, which bears his name, was conceived. The red clay teapots are completely hand-made, a compilation of calligraphy, sculpture, and plastic arts. They are found in Jiangsu and

Zhejiang mostly.

Fine clay is greasy to the touch; the texture of dry clay recalls the peeling of a pear. To make a teapot, the artisan presses and filters the clay, then leaves it for a long time, after which it is beaten into tablets. One has only to bend a tablet and cut the surplus to form the body of the teapot. In general, the body needs five or six clay tablets.

The red clay teapot is not glazed inside or outside. Of very refined form, it does not leak, and has no visible pores. Although thin, the red clay conducts the heat slowly, which is why the teapot never burns the hand. The tea infused in a red clay teapot does not deteriorate, and retains its aroma for a long time. The more it is used, the more of a patina the teapot gets and takes on the appearance of an ancient object.

According to the imagination, a craftsman can encrust silver or gold wire on the outside of a teapot, or carve patterns and Chinese characters. The artistic value of red clay teapots lies above all in the visual aesthetics, which result from the well-balanced and proportioned shape.

Black Pottery

Only since the excavations undertaken in 1928 in Longshan, Shandong Province, has it been known that the polychrome potteries do not represent the culture of the Neolithic era, but that the title belongs to the black potteries, which are fine, exquisite, and unglazed. If, 4,000 or 5,000 years ago, the revolving plate had not been used, no one could make egg shell-shaped potteries of 1 to 3 mm thickness. Undoubtedly, artisans also used the cutting knife for this kind of pottery featuring the thinness of paper, the black of ink, the brilliance of ice, and the sound of jade. In short, a chef-d'oeuvre without precedent.

The finished outlines are deposited on a wood plate to dry. Then, they undergo a second scraping. Polishing must be accomplished with organic glass tools, and with the greatest meticulousness. Then, comes the chiselling of the drawings before the last polishing and the oven baking.

Heaping and relief engraving are traditional plastic processes for decoration; they confer to these potteries classic beauty, refinement, lightness, and elegance.

Variety and Richness

These are just a few facets of Chinese culture. Discovering its elements one by one and day after day, one does not realise its richness and variety. For my part, it is when I organised my birthday party – the first in China – that I realised this richness. The guests were almost all students or teaching colleagues. Each one had tried his or her utmost to bring me a gift that warmed my heart, because these objects were mostly specialties of their provinces of origin.

To give the readers an idea, here is a list of these surprises: a painted ceramics plate; a Jingdezhen "egg shell" porcelain bowl; an interior-painted crystal bottle; a tapestry representing pandas and bamboos from Inner Mongolia (although the image belonged to the south of the country); a straw hat from Yunnan embroidered with wool, and painted; a snuff bottle (*biyanhu*) in carved bone; an enamel wicker basket from Sichuan; a pen carved with dragons and cranes (symbols of longevity); the recording of *Liang Shan Bo and Zhu Ying Tai,* classical music that I adore; a dragon-shaped horn comb from Fujian and a set of three wooden combs from Jiangsu representing historical characters; six terra cotta mini-pots; a copper incense burner from Tibet; a decorative brass teapot;

a Guizhou batik; a series of Tang tricolour horses; five bottles of wine and Chinese alcohol; a Suzhou silk scarf; a guide of China for tourists; a Beijing cloisonné bell; a collection of poems of the Tang dynasty; six comic books about the great Chinese philosophers; a set of seven cloisonnÈ bracelets; a lacquer frame for two photographs; a jade ring; an enormous cake decorated with cranes; a silk tablecloth with the "hundred children"; two house plants and cut flowers; stones of "the rain of flowers" of Nanjing; a jade old man of longevity; a carved wooden bottle from Zhejiang; a stone seal engraved with my name; a tiger-shaped pillow from Shanxi; two paintings on *xuan* paper – a landscape and a calligraphy; a bag of Ningxia wolfberries; and a dictionary of contemporary Chinese.

Wasn't I fortunate to be showered with the quintessence of Chinese culture? There were items from almost all the ethnic groups, a little of all types of crafts, from all corners of the country. It was the beginning of a collection that would never stop but it was especially the consciousness of all that I would have to discover during years. Eleven years have passed since, and I have not exhausted my curiosity yet. In addition to this list of gifts and the aspects of the Chinese culture that were detailed in this chapter, one could still mention the ball of Canton, the kites, the fans, the bamboo, and the cork articles, and so many other forms of popular art.

Conclusion

A Perfect Country?

How could China be perfect, since there is no perfect country anywhere? If China were perfect, would one hear about the large anti-corruption campaign within the government and the Party? Would there still be women kidnapped and sold as wives, and children offered to couples who cannot have their own? Would pretty young *san pei* (triple accompaniment) girls sink in the empire of alcohol, drugs, and sexual services to earn their living? Would the locations used for pornographic movies, certain kinds of massage, gambling, and other illegal activities re-open soon after having been fined? Would the courts around the country be encumbered with extortion or embezzlement? Would one be openly offered various drugs in the streets, under the eyes of policemen? Or various fake certificates and diplomas? Would one always have to wonder, when buying a CD, if it is a fraudulent product, even when one gets it in an authorised store and when the disc carries the seal of authenticity?

With my foreigner's eyes, I see two main categories among the Chinese: people born after the Cultural Revolution and their elders. The latter were moulded in obedience and discipline so well that they have lost the desire to change and the confidence of being able to succeed in it. They do not protest because "it is not worthwhile." When they have a good idea, they believe that they are abnormal and hide their thoughts rather than promote them.

Young people instead are brave. If they obey social requirements, it's only to avoid the sanctions. Deep in their hearts, they are rebellious. And ambitious. They form the group of "*mei you jingcha*" (there is no policeman), that allows them to do anything. For example, take the infractions of road regulations, such as not fastening the seat belt, passing on the red light, stopping where it is prohibited, jumping over medians, etc. If their elders are characterised by their capacity to wait, young people are full of impatience: to become wealthy immediately, to emigrate more quickly, to "seize the opportunity." They were born during or after the Cultural Revolution, but they live their best years under the "reform and opening-up" banner. The incredible progress achieved by China since 1980 is due to this catch phrase. They undergo theoretical or traditional studies, but launch themselves out in practice and trade. Or, when they graduate, they return to recycle themselves in another school's classroom. They have an open spirit and eyes. They know that the development and the future of the country rests on their shoulders, and are ready for the challenge, because they will benefit from it, and not by the spirit of generosity, sacrifice, or humanity, but prosperity. With their levers of will, they can raise the world.

If I find living in China so enthralling, it's because here, when going to bed at evening, who knows what can be found the next morning? This country is in constant evolution and stimulation. The changes are visible to the naked eye.

Since I've lived here, I have witnessed the following: the disappearance of the food rationing coupons; the opening of the stock markets; foreign restaurants (McDonald's); commercial stores (Carrefour); production establishment (Motorola) in China; the increasing ease for the Chinese to obtain a passport and travel abroad; an increase in the expression of feelings; transformation of the small State-owned stores into supermarkets and shopping centres; the advent of the "beeper," the cellular telephone, and the Internet; the proliferation of credit and debit cards, telephone cards, etc.; the mushrooming of bars and cafÈs; the end of the double monetary system (FEC and RMB); the marketing spirit and the birth of publicity along the streets, in the newspapers, and on television; the acceptance of bank loans and instalment purchases; the multiplying private cars; effective measures to protect the environment and overcome pollution; the emergence of obesity; great scientific achievements such as cloning and coding of the human genome; social reform, including sectors such as insurance; the launching of great projects such as the Three Gorges, the great development of the West and the Golmud-Lhasa railroad; the pervasion of colour printing and cartoons in newspapers; the implementation of a lottery for the benefit of sports and social welfare; the Olympic victory of Beijing; the "holiday economy;" the reform in education (paying tuition), with all the consequences; China's entry in the WTO, etc. Who says what's better? What other country has done as much? There is enough to be proud of, for China, and for the rest of the world to envy.

What Do Foreigners Say?

As I often express, in China there is no moderation: one

adapts or cracks. For some, the shock is too strong; they do not succeed in passing the bridge and prefer to turn back. But the opposite tendency is much more frequent: some young people (or less young) come to China to study language, and "fall in love" with this country. They wish at all costs to remain here. They seek housing (often illegally), employment (also), and stay in China. Others put forward their qualifications, go back to their country, and return with a valid work visa.

Many parents find that China offers splendid occasions to their children to learn not only a new language, but various forms of art or other activities that they would never master at home such as calligraphy, Peking Opera, *taiji* (one of the Chinese martial arts), and Chinese painting.

Artists and writers find that China enables them to create in peace and serenity, in addition to finding new and varied inspiration around them.

Many foreign students (Africans and Asians especially) receive a complete grant from China to study computer technology, agronomy, architecture, or music. What concerns them sometimes is the little chance they'll have, upon returning to their countries, in finding the appropriate job in their specialty.

Political refugees (Indonesia, Cambodia, Pakistan, Thailand, etc.) are often inconspicuous among the population. They do not display their status, but I can say that they are numerous among the foreign experts – those who will never go back to their countries because they would be in danger there. They are helped by China not only politically but financially, especially when they have children to send to school, which they would never be able to do with their Chinese wages.

And there are those who chose to become Chinese citizens, especially Americans, who arrived in China before Liberation, mostly. I know many foreigners (I the first) who would not refuse to take the Chinese nationality, but it is no longer possible: we would undoubtedly be too numerous, and China has its own population problems.

Way to Improve

For the Chinese, what is missing and what is needed, especially after their country entered the WTO, is, in my humble opinion, the spirit of productivity, but not any kind of production. It is not enough to do something; it should be done well. The quality of work, as much at the quality of finished products, which has improved much since I came here to live but is still not to standard, is thus an objective to be reached as soon as possible. In other words, one could say it is necessary to aim for effectiveness. The desire to innovate, accomplish, and succeed is alive in each person. What's absent is the comprehension of long-term effort. Is China ready to invest in quality for tomorrow, rather than in quantity for immediately?

About punctuality, for example: North Americans, because of their Anglo-Saxon spirit probably, much more than Europeans with a Latin spirit, are accustomed to punctuality. This virtue belongs to their work tradition. They do not try to deviate and understand that without it, nothing would function correctly. They must "punch in" at 8:00, have 30 or 50 minutes for lunch, and leave the office at the sound of the bell at the end of day, not before but often after. They are also accustomed to being productive without losing time. This is why the Chinese system seems (or may seem) to them a pure waste of time and a total confusion.

Although the task of the foreign experts in China has become much heavier with the obligation for the work units to cut expenses and provide for themselves, it is still lower than the task several among us had in our own countries. I am not still used to the idea that the Chinese need one day (if not more) of rest when they return from holidays.

Thinking of it, can one blame the Chinese to take time to laugh and relax, to cultivate friendship, to take a nap after lunch? Is it better to be effective with a sad face and mood or to refuse to be pressured and to be the slave of production? What I have just said may seem contradictory; in fact, it's a matter of finding balance. Too much on one side is not better than too much on the other. Here is the advantage of living in a country other than one's own for a certain time: without comparison, confrontation, a person does not question, does not analyse oneself, and thus, does not improve.

Westerners are so little accustomed to see people resting during day that when they see travelling merchants taking naps on their carts, or even on folding beds in the shade, in a public market, they believe they are homeless. And then, they take snapshots of "poverty" without knowing that this is *dolce vita*, instead.

The challenge posed by the WTO is much greater than the one posed by the reform and opening-up policy, because in the latter, China could proceed at its own pace, while as a WTO member, it's no longer itself that has control but the whole economic community, the level of which it must endeavour to reach without delay. This challenge is addressed especially to the 20- and 30-year-old generation. A new world has opened up to them and they must approach it with confidence, certainly, but also knowing that they are not quite ready. Therefore, their formation will have to continue, and some will even have to make a half-turn or change completely.

Individualism and Personality

What the Chinese must also work on is their individualism, as much they feel involved when a family member commits a dishonourable act, as much they are detached of any attention toward those who do not belong to their blood. It is necessary to come to a true "socialism" and – strangely – it is perhaps in Christianity that it is found the most. Often, some Chinese say they have noticed that the Christians "are good to others."

Indeed, it is especially Westerners in China who pick up an object that's fallen from a cart to give it back to its owner, who hold the door open to deliverymen with their arms filled with goods, who lift a bicycle that's fallen, or who replace the sewer lid – an open trap.

The term *kan ke* or, word for word, "to look at + invited (or witness)" well defines the indifferent attitude of too many Chinese. To look at, to see, to be a witness of what happens around but not to intervene, lend a hand, or even help in a dangerous situation. This behaviour always astonished me in this country: I who waited to see the perfect application of the slogan "all for one and one for all" in a communist society, was surprised to notice just the opposite. Each one is busy with his or her own occupation, no matter a passerby falls in the street; one closes his door and turns up the volume of the television if a neighbour hits his wife; the grandmother grabs her grandson from the gang of fighters at the end of the school day and lets the other children beat each other up. People gossip if they suspect the son of the dressmaker of making passes at young girls in his room, but would never ask the police to check what is happening. Each one keeps his or her own goats, and doesn't mind if the neighbour's fall into the well. *Kan ke,* it is looking at life as a witness, not as an actor; it is being in the audience, not on the stage.

This mentality is closely linked with the lack of personality. Did the Cultural Revolution make personality disappear? No personality, no individuality. And, when not emerging as a personality, one loses oneself in the mass, merges in the crowd, and turns to oneself, resulting in self-centredness. I think that it would be good for the Chinese to pay attention to others, in fact to themselves as social beings, as members of the society that is their life, activity, and development environment, of the society that is a network by nature.

Are Others Perfect?

For other countries in seeing China, the most urgent is to look further into their knowledge of this country that contains one-fifth of the human beings on the planet, in order to understand what occurs there. They will have to abandon initially their superiority complex that makes them believe that advanced civilisation belongs to them and that, consequently, prevents them from seeing clearly. They will have to understand that other values different from theirs not only exist, but are good, and sometimes better; and especially, to understand that each country gives itself the society and the government it wishes, which is convenient. To let China decide for itself is a principle difficult to accept for some countries, but it is the only right, humane, and respectful way.

If "from the shock of ideas spouts light," from the shock

of civilisations light can spout as well. It is thus significant that people come to know each other differently than by hear-say and travel reports. Often "misinformation" works because they're based on quick impressions, and from movies where fiction, exoticism, or single case make the rule.

More and more Westerners come to China on the one hand by curiosity or desire for the exotic, or, on the other hand, attracted by the will of checking with their own eyes the ac-curacy of their media's reports. The former, who do not seek anything special, will see only the surface, good for them! The latter, who ask themselves questions, are divided into two categories: those who search honestly and find the truth, and those who do not see anything and sink deeper in their prejudices.

My Worry for China

Seventeen years have passed since my first visit to China. More and more people, through the years, have oriented them-selves toward "money" (*xiang qian kan*) *.Where did moral values go? Confucianism has entered the museum of the spirit; the fundamental communist ideology that nourished some generations is perishing with them. Children are taught to take on the example of Lei Feng (*xue Lei Feng*), but only one day a year. This young soldier of Mao Zedong stood out by his altruism and his devotion; he died from an accident at 22 in 1962. Young people study the hero's biography as the school-children have been doing for 39 years. On March 5, they are

---

* A parenthesis here: *qian* (money) is homophonous of another qian that means "ahead." Word for word, this expression means "to look toward money" and appeared with the reform and opening up, around 1980, as a transformation of the old ideal "to look toward the future."

called to show generosity toward society; for example, by cleaning divisions on large streets or by collecting waste on the river banks or along the railways.

Orphanages and homes for the elderly (private or public) have been established; various groups of specialists and citizens work hard to protect the environment by planting trees especially on March 12, the national Tree Planting Day, or on April 6, the day of the voluntary plantation in the capital*; people donate blankets and clothing to the victims of natural disasters. However, who helps an old man get on a bus? Who yields his place to a pregnant woman? Too many people destroy public property or simply neglect it; too many citizens do not think that the dustbins along the streets exist for them too. Too many parents raise a "little emperor" rather than make their child a family member who must share the tasks and become a member of society who must assume concrete responsibilities. Instead, he or she is brought back from school, arms swinging, while the mother or grandfather is overloaded with shopping bags and the child's school bag, too.

My second concern relates to the future. Today, all seems possible in China. With modest economic means, one can set up a company. If things turn bad, one will have lost little. Several became *da kuan* (rich person) in a very short time. The national economy continues to do well; it held out at the time of the Asian financial crisis, in the 1990s, in a completely unexpected way. But one day, the curve could start to go down. What would the Chinese do, then? What would replace their feeling of plenitude, of achievement, of personal realisation, since they would have based their lives on money?

---

* In 2002, it was the Beijing 18th annual Tree Planting Day, and statistics reported that since the beginning, 37 billion trees had been planted.

I am not alone in worrying about the absence of a new national morality. It is not without reason that so many Chinese fell into the *Falun Gong* trap. When there is nothing to stick to, no ideal, one catches anything that can fill a void. The Chinese government is conscious of the problem and works on the development of a moral code, a socialist code of ethics, which will contribute to maintain (or restore) the reputation of virtue China enjoyed in the past. This task was announced on July 1, 2001, on the 80th anniversary of the foundation of the Communist Party of China. This national campaign does not aim to restore Confucianism of two millennia ago, but at extracting from it the universal and immortal principles such as "benevolence and love for others" and at applying them to today's society.

In seeking happiness and wealth, some have cultivated hedonism and forgotten the Chinese traditional virtues of modesty, tolerance, and frugality, and replaced them with ambition, selfishness, and waste. The lack of moral values has led to corruption, has blocked social development and economic reform, and even has sullied the nation's reputation. The outline of the plan for a code of ethics for the citizens includes love of the motherland, respect for laws, uprightness in acts, honesty, kindness, frugality, and devotion to work and family.

My Wish for China

When I started working in China, I wished that the country would become able not to need us foreign experts anymore, although this was going against myself. What I wished, in fact, was that China evolved to the point it would no longer be a developing country.

Let me now explain the book's title: *As Great As the World* is first my love for China that has become my new motherland; then, China itself, which has everything necessary to be appreciated as a great lady by the rest of the world.

In half a century, China has made extraordinary achievements, especially since the period of reform and opening up in 1980. Its economic development – an example for the world – may cause envy in other countries. China feeds 22% of the global population with only 7% of the arable land. It is gaining in the battle against poverty, illiteracy, disease, and infant mortality. It must still fight against natural disasters each year, and is caught in problems connected to modernisation, urbanisation, transportation, communications, energy, potable water, and pollution. It must still improve education, and develop science and technologies. But things progress, and one can see and feel the changes day after day; it is one of the main reasons why I like to live in China.

In the 11 years I've been living in Beijing, the city has changed beyond imagination. Efforts were made to improve the infrastructure, environment, and residential construction in the city and in its suburbs, so that the panorama has become unrecognisable to those who moved away for even one or two years.

I only wish that all this continues. In a city (and country) that has carried out so much in only a few years, one can only be optimistic. And optimism is a luxury today that many developed countries cannot allow themselves.

If this book helps even one person to better understand and appreciate China, as large as the world, I will not have written it in vain.

Translated from the French original version by the author, with the help of June Masuda.

图书在版编目（CIP）数据

像世界一样大= As Great as the World/(加) 李莎 (Carducci, L.) 著; 老杜绘. 北京：五洲传播出版社，2002.10
ISBN 7–5085–0096–2

Ⅰ. 像... Ⅱ. ①李... ②老... Ⅲ. 随笔–作品集–加拿大–现代–英文 Ⅳ. 1711.65

As Great as the World

像世界一样大

著　　者　李　莎 (加)
插　　图　老　杜
责任编辑　邓锦辉
封面设计　张　清
版式制作　北京天人鉴图文设计制作
出版发行　五洲传播出版社 (北京北三环中路 31 号 邮编：100088)
承　印　者　文博精品印刷有限公司
开　　本　889×1194mm　1/32
印　　张　6.5
字　　数　110 千
版　　次　2002 年 10 月第 1 版第 1 次印刷
书　　号　ISBN 7–5085–0096–2/I · 25
定　　价　26.00 元